The Jack-Roller
at Seventy

The Jack-Roller at Seventy

A Fifty-Year Follow-Up

The Jack-Roller
and
Jon Snodgrass
with
Gilbert Geis
James F. Short, Jr.
Solomon Kobrin

LexingtonBooks
D.C. Heath and Company
Lexington, Massachusetts
Toronto

Library of Congress Cataloging in Publication Data

Jack-Roller.
    The Jack-Roller at seventy.

    1. Juvenile delinquency—Illinois—Chicago—Longitudinal
studies. I. Snodgrass, Jon. II. Title.
HV9106.C4J24 1982   364.3′6′0977311   81-47825
ISBN 0-669-04912-3   AACR2

Copyright © 1982 by D.C. Heath and Company

Published simultaneously in Canada

Printed in the United States of America

International Standard Book Number: 0-669-04912-3

Library of Congress Catalog Card Number: 81-47825

To my father

—Jon

To Clifford R. Shaw

—Stanley

Contents

Acknowledgments

I would like to thank Stanley very much for writing his second auto-biography and for all the time he gave to interviews. "Stanley" is a pseudonym assigned by Clifford R. Shaw to preserve the identity of a delinquent boy who provided him with an original autobiography that was published in 1930. I have continued to use the name Stanley and spared myself the task of inventing another name, by relying on the understanding that Stanley might also be thought of as a surname. Working with Stanley has been a very gratifying experience.

Susan Lulow gave practical and emotional support without which I would never have pursued this book to completion. Gilbert Geis assisted throughout the project as an unpaid consultant and editor. I appreciate the chapters contributed by James F. Short, Jr.; Solomon Kobrin; and Gilbert Geis. Susan Spitzer-Coleman assisted editorially, Dawn Baker critiqued various drafts of the introduction, and Margie Bresnahan transcribed the tapes and typed the manuscript.

My sincerest thanks go to each of them.

Jon Snodgrass

Part I
Introduction

1 A Delinquent Boy's Own Story

Stanley, the central figure in this book, is a man in his seventies who was a *jack-roller* in the late teens and early 1920s in Chicago. A jack-roller is a robber of drunk or sleeping men, and is a term equivalent to today's mugger, particularly if the emphasis is on the helplessness of the victim. As a teenager Stanley became acquainted with Clifford R. Shaw, a graduate-student sociologist who, learning about field research, recorded Stanley's life story. The University of Chicago Press published the autobiography, along with Shaw's introduction, in 1930 as *The Jack-Roller: A Delinquent Boy's Own Story*. It was republished in paperback in 1966, an edition that had sold over 23,000 copies by the 1980s. The text thus became a classic in the field of juvenile delinquency and has been required reading for generations of sociologists training in the field.

Shaw and Stanley first met in 1921 while Shaw was occupied, in addition to his graduate studies, as a residential settlement-house worker in a Polish neighborhood. Stanley described their first meeting in a condolence letter to Shaw's wife when Shaw died in 1955:

> As a boy of twelve, I just met Cliff, back in 1921. He worked then at the Juvenile Court as well as at the settlement house on Thirty-first Street. I remember quite vividly his splendid bearing, being rugged of build, and tall of stature with a thick mane of dark hair, and quite handsome too. However, he particularly impressed me with his sincere manner and a geniality that at once captured my confidence, and that I must say was a big thing, since at that time I had spent over half my twelve years in institutions and was very much on the defensive. Instinctively I knew him as a friend.

Stanley began to write his life story when he was sixteen and recently released from the Illinois State Reformatory at Pontiac where he had served a one-year term for burglary and jack-rolling. He had first come to the attention of the police as a runaway when six and a half years old in 1913, and had been in institutions from the time he was nine years old, almost one-third his life. His record of thirty-eight arrests was not only substantial at the time Shaw intervened, but the offenses were steadily becoming more serious.

In his introductory paragraph, Shaw wrote that "the case is published to illustrate the value of the 'own story' in the study and treatment of the delinquent child."[1] The autobiography was considered an "essential pre-

liminary step" in the study of the case in order to design and implement an
effective program of rehabilitation. The story, therefore, was not an end in
itself, but a fundamental part of all the information necessary to understand and correct an offender. Shaw contextualized the life story by adding
information: an "Official Record of Arrests and Commitments"; a "Work
and School Record"; and his own essay, entitled "Social and Cultural
Background." The autobiography, as Shaw put it, was "an integral part of
the total case history."[2]

In their first interview, Shaw obtained a list of delinquencies and institutional commitments from Stanley, arranged them chronologically, and
returned them to him as a guide for his story. "He was instructed," Shaw
wrote, "to give a detailed description of each event, the situation in which it
occurred, and his personal reaction to the experience."[3] The project was interrupted, however, after a few months when Stanley was sentenced for
another year to the House of Correction on charges of burglary and jack-
rolling. It is noteworthy that Stanley perpetrated his crime during the time
he prepared his manuscript. When released, he expanded an original ten-
page statement and, at intervals over a one-year period, supplied Shaw with
additional chapters of the book. If material was relatively meager, Shaw requested some elaboration. Shaw stated that "aside from a number of cor-
rections in punctuation, the story is presented precisely as it was written by
the boy."[4]

It should be kept in mind that in attempting to rehabilitate Stanley Shaw
was dealing with an individual considered "incorrigible" by the authorities.
Read Bain described Stanley in the following terms:

> Chronic runaway at six and a half; beggar, before seven; school truant,
> before eight; shoplifter, at eight; and by this declension, in custody twenty-
> six times before the age of ten; thirty-eight times by the age of seventeen,
> including three terms in the St. Charles School for incorrigible boys and
> one year each in the Reformatory at Pontiac and the Chicago House of
> Correction. . . . If Stanley could be saved, it would seem that few such
> children need be lost.[5]

Summary of *The Jack-Roller*

Stanley was born 1 October 1907 to a Polish family in a slum section of
Chicago near the stockyards known as *Back of the Yards*. He had an older
brother and younger sister, and five older half brothers and half sisters
from his father's previous marriage. His father was employed for twenty
years as a laborer for a public-utilities company. His mother died of tuber-
culosis when Stanley was four years old, and within a year his father remarried a widow who had seven children of her own from two previous

marriages. Altogether there were fifteen children. The two parents, and six youngest children, including Stanley, lived together in a four-room basement apartment.

Stanley said that he recognized an economic necessity underlying his father's and stepmother's marriage. He bitterly resented, however, what he saw as his stepmother's cruelty to him and his brother and sister. In the company of his older stepbrother, Stanley learned to steal from railroad boxcars and from stores, often with his stepmother's approval. When he was accused by her of "corrupting" his stepbrother, he ran away from home. He slept on doorsteps and begged and stole food for four days until he was taken into custody for the first time and returned to his father.

After numerous arrests in the next few years, primarily for running away, truancy, and shoplifting, Stanley was sent to the Chicago Parental School when he was nine and remained there six months. Two months after his release, he was sent for a year and three months to the St. Charles School for Boys, and discharged when he was eleven years old. As Stanley wrote, "I went back to St. Charles after being out just twenty-four days . . . for breaking my parole."[6]

When he was twelve, Stanley was paroled to a farm in rural Illinois. After two months, he ran away to Chicago where he lived on West Madison Street, a skid-row area, for a few months until arrested as a vagrant and returned to St. Charles for another year and three months.

Paroled to his stepmother afterward, he worked sporadically at various factory jobs and frequented West Madison Street. There he met an old friend from St. Charles. They had a short-lived spree financed by a week's earnings and when broke, Stanley said:

> My buddy, being an old "jack-roller," suggested jack-rolling as a way out of the dilemma. So we started out to "put the strong arm" on drunks. We sometimes stunned the drunks by "giving them the club" in a dark place near a lonely ally. It was bloody work, but necessity demanded it—we had to live.[7]

Stanley almost always jack-rolled with a partner. He said he got "cold feet" if he tried to rob alone. When an accomplice failed to appear one day, Stanley found a job with an engraving firm instead. The vice-president informally adopted Stanley and took him to live in his home. Extremely uncomfortable in more affluent surroundings, Stanley forfeited his job and new home by absconding with some funds with which he had been entrusted.

After riding freight trains to several midwestern cities and working at menial jobs, Stanley returned to Chicago and joined a gang of four jack-rollers. "We plied our trade with howling success for two months," he wrote, and "sometimes we made as much as two hundred dollars in a single day."[8] In these assaults, which frequently victimized homosexual men,

Stanley, because of his small stature and good looks, played the role of enticer, leading prospects to a place suitably hidden for the robbery. The group also engaged in burglary. On one occasion, Stanley was identified by a victim who saw him wearing his stolen pants. Stanley was arrested and sentenced to a year in the Illinois State Reformatory at Pontiac.

As mentioned already, Stanley provided a preliminary draft for his book in the six months following his release. However, he was caught jack-rolling and sentenced to the Chicago House of Correction for another year. Shaw visited Stanley the last few weeks of his confinement, and encouraged him to get in touch when he was released. Stanley did so by going immediately to the Institute for Juvenile Research where Shaw had arranged for food, clothing, housing, and employment. The afternoon of the second day, in his new surroundings, Stanely resumed writing his life history.

Shaw reasoned that several factors were important causes of Stanley's delinquent career. First, his childhood friends and neighborhood, as well as proximity to the West Madison Street district, were thought to encourage delinquent practices. Second, the conflict with his stepmother was believed to lead to the breakdown of parental control and persistent running away; the stepmother, moreover, sanctioned delinquency. Third, Stanley's character traits of "persecution, suspicion, resistance to discipline and authority, self-justification, and a definite tendency to excuse his misconduct by means of self-pity, fatalism, and by placing the blame on other persons," also "greatly complicated his adjustment."[9] Thus there were individual, familial, and cultural aspects to his delinquent career.

Based on his understanding of the case, Shaw put into effect a five-year rehabilitation program that involved a foster-home placement, a change of neighborhoods, employment, and individual interviews. First, he found for Stanley a "sympathetic and informal" foster family in one of the nondelinquent communities in the city. Second, he obtained employment for him that was neither menial nor closely supervised. Shaw believed that Stanley needed status and autonomy, among other things, and recommended a position as a commercial salesman. Third, Shaw assisted "Stanley in making contacts with groups of young people of his age in the vicinity of his new home."[10] Fourth, "During the first two years of the period of treatment, we had personal contact with Stanley at least once a week."[11]

Stanley wrote most of his life story during the first year of the treatment period. In the final chapter, he described a personal inability to adapt to salesmanship, a difficulty that led him to take either factory or clerical positions. Usually he was fired from these jobs for arguments or physical fights with personnel and supervisors, inevitably over matters of authority. At this time Stanley seems to have had trouble working both alone and with others. Shaw noted that it was Stanley's "egocentric personality" that made adjustment difficult, although this idea was not developed. Stanley was also unable to complete night courses in high school.

At the end of the second year, for reasons that are not entirely clear, Stanley managed to become a door-to-door appliance salesman, and wrote "I. . . .found it to be the most fascinating type of work I had ever done."[12] The autobiographical material concerning this development in treatment, however, is meagerly described in that the last four years are covered in a matter of paragraphs. For example, two and a half years after release from the House of Correction, Shaw quotes Stanley, "With my success in selling came a feeling of confidence in my ability to get along in the business world."[13] Four years later Stanley commented, "I am now settled in the warmth and congenial atmosphere of my own home with my wife and child."[14] Generally, the end of the autobiographical section gives the impression that Stanley's situation improved rapidly once he was suitably employed. Shaw concluded his "Summary of Case and Social Treatment" with the statement:

> More than five years have elapsed since Stanley was released from the House of Correction. During this period there has not been a recurrence of any delinquent behavior. Furthermore, he has developed interests and a philosophy of life which are in keeping with the standards of conventional society. While it is impossible to analyze all the factors which have been instrumental in producing these modifications in his interests and conduct, it may be assumed that they were due, in large part, to changes in group relationships. In other words, his present behavior trends, interests, and philosophy of life have developed as a product of his participation in the life of conventional social groups.[15]

In addition to his own contribution of three chapters, Shaw included a "Brief Summary of Clinical Findings." This report was based on a medical and psychological examination by William Healy, a well-known Chicago physician and criminologist, performed when Stanley was almost eight years of age. Healy's diagnosis in 1915 was: "a) bad neighborhood; b) bad influence in family and poor parental control; c) bad companions." His prognosis was: "Outlook good if constructive work is done in the case."[16] Shaw's intervention began about ten years later.

Shaw also included a "Discussion" chapter by Ernest W. Burgess, a famous University of Chicago social psychologist. Burgess was the first of many observers to note that Shaw's treatment plan emphasized changing social circumstances as contrasted with changing personality. Shaw recognized this tendency when he referred to it as a program of social treatment." Burgess described it as a case of "transplantation,"[17] and stated that "Mr. Shaw's final choice of the occupation of commercial salesman showed his ingenuity in adapting treatment to the traits of personality."[18] Burgess also believed that, "The transformation of Stanley from a criminal to a law abiding citizen was a change in social type . . . " and that the treatment process was a "brilliant success."[19]

Over the years, *The Jack-Roller* has been discussed frequently in journals and textbooks. It has become the focus for several special studies whose authors reflect a variety of viewpoints ranging from the methodological to the clinical.[20] Appearing almost fifty years after Shaw's and Burgess's, this book consists of an autobiographical sequel and a series of interviews. In a section of analyses, three prominent criminologists offer their observations about the case.

The autobiography itself covers the remainder of Stanley's life through approximately 1980. The interviews provide a somewhat more intense view of his situation during the late 1970s, when the sequel was written and edited. In his oral style Stanley tends to be more simple, direct, and authentic as contrasted with his written style. As one of the longest individual follow-up studies and most extensively studied individuals in the history of the social sciences, Stanley's case provides an excellent empirical opportunity for the comparison, assessment, and discussion of criminological theory and practice.

Notes

1. Clifford R. Shaw, *The Jack-Roller: A Delinquent Boy's Own Story,* 2nd ed. (Chicago: University of Chicago Press, 1966), p. 1.
2. Ibid., p. 2.
3. Ibid., p. 23.
4. Ibid., p. 47.
5. Read Bain, "Review of *The Jack-Roller: A Delinquent Boy's Own Story,*" *The Annals of the American Academy of Political and Social Science* 151 (1930):285.
6. Shaw, *The Jack-Roller,* p. 72.
7. Ibid., p. 85.
8. Ibid., p. 97.
9. Ibid., p. 165
10. Ibid., p. 166.
11. Ibid., pp. 166-167.
12. Ibid., p. 181.
13. Ibid., pp. 181-182.
14. Ibid., p. 182.
15. Ibid., p. 183.
16. Ibid., p. 199.
17. Ibid., p. 195.
18. Ibid., p. 196.
19. Ibid., p. 194.

20. John Dollard, *Criteria for the Life History: With an Analysis of Six Notable Documents* (New York: Peter Smith, 1949); Harold Finestone, *Victims of Change: Juvenile Delinquents in American Society* (Greenwood Press: Westport, Connecticut, 1976); Harold Finestone, "The Delinquent and Society: The Shaw and McKay Tradition," in James F. Short, Jr., ed., *Delinquency, Crime and Sociology* (Chicago: University of Chicago Press, 1976); Stuart A. Rice, "Hypotheses and Verifications in Clifford R. Shaw's Studies of Juvenile Delinquency," in Stuart A. Rice, ed., *Methods in Social Science: A Case Book* (Chicago: University of Chicago Press, 1931), pp. 549-565; James F., Short, Jr. *Delinquency, Crime and Society* (Chicago: University of Chicago Press, 1976).

A Fifty-Year Follow-Up

I first became acquainted with *The Jack-Roller* in the early 1960s as an undergraduate studying sociology at the University of Maryland. I remember being particularly fascinated by the aspect of the story Howard S. Becker refers to as "the conversation between the classes." The volume described a social reality that I thought existed but was rarely mentioned in my texts and courses. Shaw's example, that sociology might be relevant to my own experience, was an inspiration to me. I believed the story was authentic, and Shaw's causal analysis and treatment plan were important. At the same time, however, I believed that Shaw omitted from his theory many of the political and economical factors that seemed obvious to me in the story. Nevertheless, I regarded the life-history approach as fundamental in the development of criminological theory.

In the early 1970s, as a doctoral candidate at the University of Pennsylvania, I wrote a dissertation on the intellectual history of American criminology. It ____ biographical sketches and critiques of the works of several major criminological ____ Healey; Clifford R. Shaw and Henry D. ____, Edwin H. Sutherland, and Sheldon and Eleanor Glueck.[1] In the ____ to demonstrate that a middle-class bias existed in crim ____ related to the homogeneous backgrounds of the theorists ____ apply concepts from the work of C. Wright Mills ____ sociology ____ I was trying also to make available for crim ____ approximated Robert A. Nisbet's *The Sociolo ____ of Sociological Thought* ____

During my ____ interested in locating Stanley, primarily as a means of ____ getting ____ information about Shaw's background and think ____. While gathering material on Shaw, I interviewed his wife, Hetta, and their son, Bill. One afternoon Bill was on the verge of giving me Stanley's current address when Hetta advised him that to do so might violate their commitment to protect Stanley's anonymity. Accordingly, we arranged for Bill to write Stanley about my interest and to send him my address. In this way Stanley could decide for himself whether or not to become involved. For a long time no reply came from Stanley.

I completed my dissertation, obtained the Ph.D., and moved to Los Angeles to teach in the California State University system in the early 1970s. I wrote to Bill Shaw several times urging him to remind Stanley of my interest. At one point, I checked out a Los Angeles address for Stanley, kindly provided by James Bennett, author of *Oral History and Delinquency: The Rhetoric of Criminology.*[3] The landlord of the apartment building remembered Stanley but had not seen him for several years. Consequently, I set this project aside and turned my attention to other research interests. Eventually, however, I received a letter from Stanley dated 31 December 1975. It occurred to me that the decision to write may have been one of Stanley's New Year's resolutions. He wrote:

Dear Sir:

Some time ago, in fact several years to be more exact, Mr. William Shaw referred your name as being interested in a sequel to the book his father wrote, *The Jack-Roller,* by the principal "Stanley," the above person, who is now writing you this letter.

I trust that this message shall still find you at the above university which he mentioned. If this reaches you, I would like to hear from you regarding the possibility of writing a sequel, only if it be of value in terms of the common good, of your profession and those unfortunate youngsters like I once was many years ago.

Any monetary consideration is of secondary importance as far as I am concerned. I have fond and deep appreciation for not only Mr. Clifford R. Shaw, my once dearest friend and his entire family, whom I knew intimately for over fifty years, but also to the many associates that I encountered during these years, and found them, mostly, sincere and dedicated people that devoted their lives to studying the problems of the delinquent child.

If it is still to *your* interest in collaborating with me for a contribution to a cause which belongs in the present of attempting to determine the causes and possible alleviation of this problem, I assure you that I am sincere in extending whatever small assistance I may be able to offer.

I am usually at home mornings and throughout the day, and may be contacted at that time.

Trusting this finds you, and hoping for a response, I remain.

Yours truly,
/s/ Stanley

PS: Please treat this confidentially.

Happy New Year!

Soon we had dinner. That we lived in the same geographical area was sheer coincidence, but that his apartment was in East Los Angeles, less than twenty minutes from the university where I taught, was too good to be true. I found Stanley an alert, handsome, seventy-year-old man who was eager to participate in a follow-up. He referred to himself as a retired businessman, recently remarried, who lived in an apartment in Echo Park, a Mexican-American section of the city. His new situation seemed both to make it possible for and to motivate him to contact me. As a "tribute to Shaw," he explained, he wanted a follow-up study to show how happy and well adjusted his life had finally become. He had "learned the value of friends, family and good books," as he put it. It might be conjectured that Stanley waited to get in touch with me until he felt he had achieved the set of life circumstances that coincided with those expected of him by Shaw as described in the conclusion to the first story.

Over dinner we discussed two possible follow-up methods; tape-recorded interviews or a second autobiography. Stanley felt himself incapable of writing another book and, as a result, I thought I would try to prepare a journal article that might incorporate interviews. We, therefore, tentatively agreed to tape a series of sessions. In the meantime, I submitted a research proposal to the Crime and Delinquency Section of the National Institute of Mental Health, asking for funds to examine Shaw's hypothesis concerning the jack-roller's reformation at the end of the five-year treatment period. I was awarded a small grant (number RO1MH29452-01) that allowed me one-quarter's release time from teaching, while Stanley received $1,000 for his contribution. We had our first discussion in the winter of 1976, and began the actual project in the summer of 1977.

When we first met in the summer, Stanley surprised me with a six-inch by nine-inch handwritten notebook that consituted the initial installment on his second autobiography. In this instance, I thought Stanley attempted to fulfill what he thought were my expectations of him. The notebook, I later calculated, contained approximately four thousand words, most of which were illegible. The practice of giving a gift, especially at the outset of a relationship, I recognized subsequently as a personal habit of Stanley's. In his first story, for example, he initiated friendships by offering money, drinks, fruit, or anything else at hand. Because of Stanley's handwriting, I asked him to dictate the notebook on tape.

Also in this session, Stanley divulged the information now contained in chapter 7 concerning his institutionalization during the 1940s in the Illinois State Hospital at Kankakee. He explained that he had been informed by his mother-in-law about the marital infidelities of his wife. This information confirmed some of his worst fears, and he went to her apartment in a rage. They argued he said and he left hurriedly.

Apparently, she called the police and accused Stanley of threatening her life. He was picked up by the police as he wandered the streets barefooted and in a daze (see chapter 7). In a brief hearing, a judge sent him to the State Hospital for confinement. While in this institution, as a result of an argument and fight with another inmate, Stanley was placed on the hydrotherapy ward, reserved exclusively for violent patients (see chapter 8).

In revealing his commitment to a mental institution to me at the very beginning of our discussions, I thought Stanley was being extremely honest. Unavoidably, I also wondered about the implications of this information for Shaw's treatment conclusion. Stanley became quite emotional in recollecting this experience, and at the end of the session it seemed like a gift had been exchanged for my friendship.

Stanley further indicated in this session that his wife had used *The Jack-Roller* to thwart his efforts to gain release from Kankakee by actually showing the book to the authorities. The idea that his wife was ultimately responsible for his original confinement and subsequent retention in this institution is shown in the following quote:

> She threw *The Jack-Roller* book at me. The law in Illinois was that if a woman wants to keep you there, all she has to say is that "I fear for my life, he wants to kill me."

> She also made the statement to the police that I threatened her with a knife, which was absolutely untrue. We were discussing things at the dining room table and there might have been a knife on the table—like knives are on tables. But I didn't go and get that knife to threaten her—it happened to be there. She used this as an excuse to have me locked up.

When I heard the content of the notebook after Stanley had dictated it on tape, the results seemed very disappointing. The material was impersonal and disorganized, quite unlike the vividly coherent style of the first story. Hardly any of this material has been retained except a few paragraphs placed in the final chapter. (Today, I believe I was a little naive concerning the kind of personal support Stanley needed in order to accomplish his self-imposed assignment.) I encouraged him to write more directly about his own experiences and develop the story in chronological sequence, beginning with his involvement with Shaw, which coincided with his release from the House of Correction in 1925. I left a tape recorder with him at his apartment and asked that he continue to dictate the notebook. We met every other week for several hours in the afternoon during this period while he continued to record his second story privately.

During this same period in the summer of 1977, Stanley also decided to return to work as a salesman of music lessons, an occupation from which he had considered himself retired for ten years. He felt he needed extra money to finance a trip with his second wife "Sonia," to visit his children and grandchilden, one of whom lived in England. Part of Stanley's motivation seemed to be a desire to display his new domestic situation to his relations. Thus, Stanley's outreach to me and dedication to the sequel, were parts of a more general development in his life at this time that also included marriage and reemployment.

Possibly, Stanley also was interested in escaping a financial dependency on Sonia for the larger household expenditures. She recently had purchased a stereo for him and paid for an automobile to enable him to get around and return to work. He repeatedly told me that he intended to repay these debts with his prospective earnings. He also indicated that her bigger income and savings gave her an advantage in their relationship (see chapter 15). Sonia's finances seemed to put Stanley in a subordinate status that threatened his manhood, a difficulty similarly experienced in his first marriage (see chapter 6). Returning to work appeared to be a way of trying to correct his feelings of powerlessness in the relationship.

Stanley's decision to return to work created a great deal of stress, (see chapters 16 and 17). Sonia began to complain about the amount of time he was away from home. They quarreled, and he struck her on one occasion (see chapter 15). Stanley moved out and Sonia initiated divorce proceedings. Although they reconciled some of their differences within a few months and continued to see each other as friends, Stanley felt that Sonia was unwavering in her determination to obtain a divorce. Stanley was more ambivalent about the divorce, as the interview material seems to show. Altogether they lived as a married couple for eighteen months.

My relationship with Stanley was not established very firmly, and our work had not progressed very far when their separation took place. It seriously interrupted our process; for more than a month I lost contact with him and thought our project probably was finished. When Stanley finally telephoned me, he was living alone and had moved from East Los Angeles to a furnished apartment in the downtown area. He told me that he had written another portion of his life story and that he was prepared to dictate it.

In the past I had asked Stanley to dictate the written material by himself so that our time together might be used for interview purposes. This time, and thereafter, I listened to the dictations in his presence and interviewed him afterward. My attention to Stanley greatly facilitated our working relationship and improved the quality of the material (as evidenced by the fact that it constitutes chapter 1). We met once a week for two to three hours in the afternoon through the end of 1977 to tape the story and record the interviews.

Often as I arrived for a session, Stanley would be waiting outside the apartment building or returning quickly from a nearby park (see chapter 19), in order to escort me into his new security hotel. If I was a moment or two late, he referred to me jokingly as "the delinquent." His studio quarters were very neat and clean. He shopped and cooked for himself and was entirely independent and self-sufficient. He had lived this way for years, he said. Before we began to talk each time, he graciously provided some refreshment, and at times I brought something for us too.

Stanley's tall, slender build and full, white hair, of medium length, parted to one side, gave him a handsome, even stately, appearance. He fre-

quently wore a blue and red checked leisure suit. He was diet conscious and
in good health, except that occasionally he seemed to lose his balance while
standing or walking, which he attributed to an inner-ear problem. Several
chipped false front teeth were the only flaw in his appearance and he mentioned many times that he planned to have them fixed through a state-
operated medical-insurance program. On occasion we discussed the possibility of taking photographs. Stanley was tempted, but in the end, out of a
concern for protecting the reputations of his children's families, he decided
to remain incognito.

Before the end of the year, Stanley moved back to the neighborhood
where his second wife lived (the neighborhood where we first met). He
explained the reason for his move:

> The manager was real nice after I gave him notice. I didn't argue with him,
> I just slipped it under his door. We had some words later. I said, "I hope
> you found the notice. You know what you can do with it." He said,
> "Don't get smart." He didn't like it.
>
> These two brothers who fixed my car were up there in mechanic's clothes.
> They didn't look too good as far as prestige is concerned, but he didn't
> know that, he probably thought they were a couple of bums out of the
> park.
>
> Another guy, a chess player I've known for years, has a wild look in his
> eye, but is a real nice fellow, the manager thought he was drunk. My friend
> was waiting for me outside, he wanted to get in. He had called me and I had
> said, "Alright, come on over." I never anticipated (laughs) . . . Oh man, I
> really got hot then. He told my friend, "Get the hell out of here, you're
> drunk," and kind of pushed him around, at least verbally. I didn't like it.
> So I showed him—I gave notice.

By the time I visited Stanley in December of 1977 for interview eight
(chapter 21), he and Sonia were living together again:

> Our separation, that was just an aberration. I messed up, you know—
> pushing myself like a damn fool as though I was twenty-years-old again.
> I'm so emotionally constituted that I can't stand any undue strain—it's
> conducive to emotional outbursts. But, we haven't had any trouble. It was
> a regrettable thing that happened.

The final interview (chapter 22) was recorded in the spring of the
following year when Stanley had been attacked outside his and Sonia's
apartment as he was returning late one night from a round of cards. He
was knocked down, his wallet taken, and his hip broken in several places.
He was hospitalized for a couple of weeks (during which time I visited
him), and on crutches for several months. Sonia also participated in this
interview. Aside from infrequent telephone calls, the last one in the fall of

1980, this was my final personal contact with "the jack-roller." I informed him in the spring of 1981 that Lexington Books had decided to publish his sequel.

In the preparation of Stanley's second story, a considerable amount of editorial work has been done. The major cuts have been with regard to Stanley's reliance on redundant vocabulary. Although a pretentious literary style may be more characteristic of Stanley's generation, this tendency also seems intended to impress the reader with the author's eruidition and linguistic ability. Traces of this practice remain in the text. The vocabulary, however, is entirely Stanley's, as are the content and sequence of paragraphs. While I have tried to maintain the spirit of the first volume, the organization into chapters and the titles of the chapters are the editor's. The autobiography itself tends to cover Stanley's past while the interviews concentrate on his current life situation. These materials, together with this chapter, might be considered three new sources of information on the Jack-Roller. Hopefully they may serve as a foundation for a more complete discussion of the implication of this case history for criminological theory, research, and correction.

Notes

1. Jon Snodgrass, "The American Criminological Tradition: Portraits of the Men and Ideology in a Discipline," (Ph.D. diss. University of Pennsylvania, 1972). Two parts were published as articles: "Clifford R. Shaw and Henry D. McKay: Chicago Criminologists," *British Journal of Criminology* (1975); and "The Criminologist and His Criminal: The Case of Edwin H. Sutherland and Broadway Jones," *Issues in Criminology* (1973). The latter was also a follow-up of a kind of case study.

2. Robert A. Nisbet, *The Sociological Tradition* (New York: Basic Books, 1966); Lewis A. Coser, *Master of Sociological Thought* (New York: Harcourt Brace Jovanovich, 1971).

3. James Bennett, *Oral History and Delinquency: The Rhetoric of Criminology* (Chicago: University of Chicago Press, 1981).

Part II
Autobiographical Sequel

3 The Big Band House

The recording of my life story, *The Jack-Roller,* published by the University of Chicago Press in 1930, under the authorship of Clifford R. Shaw, described my experiences from the earliest childhood period until the year of my marriage. Since this version was subtitled *The Delinquent Boy's Own Story,* my good friends Jon Snodgrass and Gilbert Geis have encouraged me to relate the subsequent fifty years of my life experiences. These learned gentlemen are well qualified to evaluate the sociological merit of my statements. Personally, as a layman, I view my autobiography as of little significance and entertain no illusions about its intrinsic value. I am willing, however, to record it for scientific interest. In doing so, I also wish to honor the memory of Clifford R. Shaw, who unfailingly counseled me throughout my earlier years.

Chicago, in the early 1900s, was regarded as the city of opportunity due to its central geographical location and phenomenal growth. The sprawling area of the Chicago Stockyards, about one-mile square, contained a maze of slaughter houses and pens. An endless procession of switch engines busily and boisterously emitted soot, grime, and smoke that produced a dark umbrella over the southwest section of the city. Into this bustle of industry I was born in October 1907, and here I spent my early years. I was a true native of Back of the Yards, since we lived within its very precincts.

The spring of 1925 found me a patient in the prison infirmary of the Chicago House of Correction, a place others often referred to as *The Bridewell* or *Bandhouse.* The latter appellation probably derived from an almost total prohibition on ordinary privileges such as smoking, which was banned until recently. This prison consisted of three cell blocks, the first was built well before the Civil War and once housed Confederate prisoners of war.

The South Cell House had four large galleries of cubicles scarcely more than four- by five-feet square. Each cell had two bunks. Sanitary provisions consisted of an iron bucket for a toilet, and a narrow tin cannister wired to the cell bars for drinking water. The corridor had a long trough where water spouted from perforated holes of piping, which allowed morning ablutions to be wiped away with a towel issued once a week to each inmate. This primitive structure at this time housed perhaps a thousand prisoners. Overcrowding forced up to four prisoners into each cell; two used the floor for sleeping. An overpowering stench emanated from this cell block, its effects extending to the outer precincts, and added to the general fetidness of the prison atmosphere.

After a breakfast of plain oatmeal, bread, and chicory, a procession of men carried their slop buckets from their cells to a large latrine well where they were emptied and rinsed of their contents.

As a trusty, I was quartered in the third cell block, called the West Cell House, a recent addition. It boasted of private roomy cell space, a comfortable bed, and all the modern plumbing conveniences. I was originally assigned to the prison tailor shop. Through the influence of my partner, who was involved in the same offense, I had the good fortune to be selected a *runner* in the deputy's office. This stroke of good luck allowed me a measure of freedom. I covered the entire prison in my various errands and enjoyed the fresh air and sunshine, quite a luxury, comparatively speaking.

One of my duties was to cut, into approximately one-inch squares and issue once a week plugs of prison-made tobacco, shipped from the State prison farm in Vandalia, Illinois. Needless to say, my arrival in each department with a supply of this welcome treat represented the only concession by a hard and uncompromising administration. There was always a surplus sufficient for me to trade for smoking tobacco and perhaps a package of the then contraband cigarettes that were smuggled in somehow. Matches, too, were banned. Those having any supply would prudently split the sticks to obtain their maximum use.

The prison kitchen personnel did a thriving business in filching potatoes, which were fried in grease with a piece of meat, wrapped in a paper package, and referred to as *lumps*. These were usually exchanged for tobacco. Of this contraband I had my share, but there existed no recourse to such things as eggs, milk, or fruit, so essential to a balance diet. Thus my susceptibility to arthritis, influenza, and the almost fatal effects of pneumonia could be attributed largely to the prison diet. Several years were required to fully recuperate from this siege. Remarkably, however, I never had a recurrence of the arthritic condition; the body somehow had developed an immunity that to the present day has left me free from its debilitating ravages.

Since the deputy's office adjoined the solitary punishment cells, I often witnessed the summary disposition of those who broke discipline. Placed in *the hole* for varying periods, some required hospital treatment as a result of the belaboring of the heavy wooden clubs wielded by guards such as Iron Jaw, who ran the quarry, and Pickhandle Slim, who headed the brickyard and clay-hole gang. The *ticket* describing the infraction provided no avenue of appeal from the closing of the heavy doors, a Stygian darkness, and a bread and water diet once each day. Though tight restrictions prevailed, I found the majority of guards reasonable in their supervision. The complete lack of recreation, the poor housing, and the inadequate diet were a form of punishment in themselves, however.

The daily arrival of a large bus, usually packed to overflowing capacity, disgorged a motley array of derelicts. Many were chronic alcoholics, fined for various amounts and sentenced up to a year.

The remainder were criminal types who had escaped indictment by the grand jury through the leniency of the court, which had reduced a more serious charge to the status of a misdemeanor. Actually, some of these more vicious offenders would be given a year's sentence together with a fine of $1,000 and costs of $6.50. Failure to pay this fine meant almost three years of servitude. Often I heard this type declare they would rather have a longer sentence in the relatively friendly confines of the state penitentiary. With this attitude I quite agree, for in the vernacular of the prisoner, the Bridewell was a *tough joint* in which to do time.

The criminal group was represented by a goodly number of young and vicious types of burglars and stickup men, many of whom would be candidates eventually for the *stir,* the penitentiary at Joliet. Their conversations invariably concerned their determination to pursue their ambitions in a criminal career upon release. In the interim, however, their behavior was well restricted by the rigidness of a routine that brooked no compromise with any deviation of the rules.

In the shower room each prisoner divested his clothing, which was placed in a large burlap sack and then deloused. Amazingly, the hot shower and the often misfitting prison denims, transformed many of these grime-encrusted derelicts into persons of apparent respectability. Thus some credence was lent to the large sign in this room that displayed the legend "Cleanliness is the next to Godliness."

A work assignment to one of the various departments was rapidly given: shoe shop, laundry, tailor shop, quarry, and clay pit. The elderly and infirm were usually assigned to lay-in cells. Some individuals required a short period in the prison infirmary to recuperate from injuries suffered during exposure in sleeping in streets and alleys and injuries inflicted by marauders who preyed upon them. Some, too, had imbibed *derail* or wood alcohol, or other noxious liquids.

Indeed, I still vividly recall the atmosphere of West Madison Street whence the alcoholics came. A pall arose from the fumes of the poisonous concoctions, which were available for as little as twenty-five cents the half pint. The common scene on Skid Row streets was an unbelievable number of inebriates lying in sidewalks and alleys, and a constant procession of patrol wagons scarcely making any appreciable dent in their efforts to pick up the human debris that defied a lasting solution through ever-recurring numbers.

The Volstead Act, noble in purpose, was ineffectual for it lacked enforcement and opened wide the door for the entrance of characters like Al Capone, Louie Alterie, Bugs Moran, and numerous others. The demand would not be denied and provided a fabulous source of income that in dimension made the earnings of our largest corporations dwarfs in comparison. Local law enforcement clandestinely encouraged the development of a huge new empire by accepting bribes. Much of the political system was infected with greed and virtually aided and abetted the growth of the under-world.

Space, I feel, should be devoted to describing a character in the House of Correction whom we called simply and rather fondly Old Bill. He represented the epitome of the confirmed chronic alcoholic. His com-mitments to the institution numbered in the hundreds and often only a day separated his releases and arrivals. His term covered over forty years of his life. Old Bill was always assigned to taking care of the solitary quarters. Now infirm and almost blind from past countless bouts with John Barleycorn, he continued his faithful duties of keeping the hole in order. Unrequited, too, was his devotion to the demon rum, or rather a bootleg variety of highly questionable quality. There was something about him that suggested a redoubtable character with a dignity all his own. One might easily regard him as the dean of alcoholics who made the Bridewell his home.

As the day of my release approached, my interest in books increased, together with an accompanying desire to meet life's challenges with a new determination. Clearly, I was becoming more aware that a precarious ex-istence in my return to the streets held no promise, and I had acquired a more than ordinary aversion to further incarceration. At seventeen years of age, I discovered that I had spent well over half of these years in jails and in-stitutions.

4 Prospects

My term in the House of Correction was nearing its end when I was visited by Clifford R. Shaw, whom I had known a few years before as a settlement worker. As I recall, the beginning of *The Jack-Roller* took place after my release from Pontiac in 1923, which was interrupted by the sentence to the House of Correction in 1925. Shaw broached a continuation of the story I began some few years before, and I agreed to cooperate. He also offered to assist with some clothing, which I welcomed. His pleasing personality found me quite receptive, and I noted his virile and commanding appearance, which further increased my respect for him. As he left, he reminded me to get in touch with him when I was released and again offered to help in any way he could.

Never before had prison doors swung open to my relief as on that bright morning in June. With the singing of the birds, the outside world seemed like a fairyland. Finding a welling response within me, I vowed never again to deprive myself of freedom. No allure remained to resume a career of crime. I was determined to find my place in the free world. The few years before my marriage were critical in that I was making a sincere effort to turn from my old antisocial habits, in the process facing the problems of this new adjustment.

Arriving at my stepmother's, a few miles from the old home Back of the Yards, I found her new place more spacious and pleasant, and, surprisingly, her reception was warm and friendly. To an extent this made me rather uncomfortable, for I was at a loss to cope with one that had made my life so miserable in my early childhood. I had disturbing reservations about her sudden changes. Her younger children, about my age, still with her, also received me reasonably well.

When my half brother from my father's first marriage, invited me to live with him, I must confess that I was greatly relieved to absent myself from my stepmother's presence and hospitality. In spite of her cruelties to my brother and sister in the past, she did make me aware of the almost too difficult situation she faced in raising the large brood of children, and in my now maturing mind I acknowledged a degree of credit. Yet it was utterly impossible for me to extend any gesture of affection, being content to show a measure of respect only.

Living with my brother seemed preferable and I was conscious that the blood relationship would establish an acceptance for which I deeply yearned. The curiosity of being without a family in my early years left a void that gave me a desire to know of its blessings. I was certain that I missed something very necessary and felt my loss more keenly and envied the lot of those having parents. Belonging to a family seemed like such a wonderful thing. In my isolation I constantly experienced a desolate feeling of loneliness. Therefore, I seized the opportunity to belong to my brother's household.

Thus, in living with my brother I hoped to recapture a remnant of the family ties that so escaped me in childhood. In his community, called Bridgeport (also the home of the late Mayor Edward J. Daley), I hoped to take root and become an accepted member of the family. My brother and I trudged the streets seeking a job, and he regaled me with his wartime experiences as an artillery man in World War I. I might add that another brother, who also lived with him, served honorably for seven years in the navy and army of occupation in Germany. Their service proves that there was no lack of patriotism in our family. I found a job doing light assembly work and happily assumed gainful employment.

One day I accepted an invitation to take an auto trip to St. Charles with a small group that included Shaw. I was interested in returning to the scene of my childhood days so filled with repression. One might say that I was attending an alumni meeting with myself.

Returning from the trip to St. Charles at a rather late hour in the night, I found my brother's home in darkness. He answered my knock with a brief tirade, ordered me to leave, shut the door in my face, and abruptly ended my short stay. He misunderstood my late arrival as an indication of falling into old ways. I was hurt, for I found no fault with him, he was kind and always treated me well. The full reality of being a pariah was a thought hard to bear.

I telephoned Shaw, explained my predicament, and was urged to come to his apartment which he shared with a young college professor, Leonard Cottrell, an altogether engaging person. The next few days I spent in the pleasant company of these two cultured people.

I appreciated the luxury of what was really a modest apartment but represented a distinct contrast to what I had known in my neighborhood. I was particularly attracted to the furnishings, which indicated more than a casual taste. An assortment of articles, including many books, made me conscious and fascinated with the general atmosphere of refinement. The cordial hospitality made me feel a part of it.

The natural and simple charm of Shaw's great and humane personality proved over the ensuing years to be genuine. He probably took note of how much I enjoyed the area in which his apartment was located, quite close to Lake Michigan and marked by respectable homes and modern apartment buildings, for he asked if I would like to live in such surroundings. My response was more than enthusiastic. After a few days he found quarters for me a stone's throw from the Midway that embraced the campus of the University of Chicago, and a few blocks from the broad expanse of beautiful Jackson Park.

Shaw introduced me to Mrs. Smith, who owned a small, two story home. This rather unassuming woman led me upstairs and showed me the room I could rent at a modest price. Though her home was not luxurious, there was an unmistakable genteel character about her that was suggested by the books and piano. My reaction at the outset was a sense of humility, in that I regarded myself as an intruder. I felt particularly guilty of my past record of prison life.

At Mrs. Smith's there were no restrictions placed on my coming and going and, though I was gently chided at times for not returning at reasonable hours, this is as far as it went. My late hours were usually on weekends, however, when I spent a good deal of time at a relative's candy store where I learned to play pinochle and penny-ante poker.

Shaw was able to place me with the telegraph company, and I was given an opportunity to be trained as an operator. My ineptitude was not from a lack of application or desire. My finger reflexes were still affected by the arthritis that precluded the required progress. However, I was given employment with simple duties that were pleasant in the main building that housed the central system.

Since Shaw lived but a short distance away, I was afforded many opportunities for visits that were very helpful in solidifying my adjustment to this new life. The three years after my release from the Bridewell, until I married, were not exactly a perfect example of adjustment since I held a number of jobs in that period. My main problem seemed to consist of a particular sensitivity to resentment, whether due to real or fancied causes, that aroused within me combative tendencies. These feelings resulted in fist fights that meant dismissal from employment.

I made an attempt to continue my education, taking two subjects in night school. When I enumerated the years necessary to complete my high-school degree, however; I lost patience.

Too much cannot be said of Shaw's influence in my apparent adjustment, and this applies also to his good friend Henry D. McKay. What particular factor was responsible for the change that took place within me is an appropriate question. Perhaps a more mature attitude and outlook are relevant. Also, I was growing weary of coping with institutional life, especially after the term in the House of Correction.

Further, my interest in the opposite sex was far more absorbing than in the past and added to my general adjustment. Maturity was approaching and life seemed to hold some promise.

My apparent adjustment, however, still revealed a glaring inability on my part regarding relationships with others, especially those with whom I worked. I was often unduly sensitive, carrying a chip on my shoulder, particularly if I fancied myself being imposed upon. I reacted aggressively at critical times, which resulted in dismissal such as occurred at the telegraph company. My regret was overwhelming, for the loss of this position left me isolated again. The broken security of my routine gave me more pause to ponder my indiscretions.

Through the intercession of another roomer at Mrs. Smith's, during the very first year after my release from the House of Correction in 1925, it became my good fortune to work in the laboratory of a large hospital. As I was utterly lacking in any training to qualify me for the exacting requirements of technical work, my tasks were limited to menial ones.

Among my duties were assisting the pathologist in the course of his postmortem operations, by placing the body on the dissection table and laying out the instruments in readiness. I must confess that I could never overcome my fear and foreboding on viewing the stark aspects of the rigid corpse that once was animated and now represented a grim and final oblivion.

I mention this experience for I wish to follow the same process of dissection of my feelings, my experiences, and the events that took place in the ensuing fifty years. I will attempt to expose my past to the best of my memory and weigh its significance. Just as the laboratory technician carries out the various tests to enable the physician to determine the diagnosis of his patient, I shall try to record my attitudes, allowing the sociological critics to draw their own conclusions about my personality and personal development.

I was reasonably happy working at the hospital. I was impressed by the special abilities of the people and marveled at their required educational background. By admiring them, I found within me the desire to go to night school if I expected to move ahead in the future. Mrs. Smith planted the seed of curiosity by teaching me that knowledge is power. This gentle and refined woman unassumingly and unobtrusively sparked a flame within my soul. I regret greatly today that I failed to avail myself of her excellent counsel.

Mrs. Smith's son was about my age. We became friends and spent much time together. He introduced me to the intricacies of chess, among other things. I enjoyed his company but felt very self-conscious and inadequate in measuring up to him. It was strange, but refreshing, to be placed so suddenly within this family and cultural background. I felt like a pig coming out of its sty to invade the secret precincts of the parlor. The sordidness and savagery of my past environment made me aware of the great need to conform in order to establish legitimacy.

Unfortunately, shortly after I began living there, this boy met with a tragic accidental death in the home. To put it mildly, this was a terrible blow to Mrs. Smith. In spite of her great grief, she presented a brave appearance, managing somehow to conceal the deepest sorrow that only a mother for her lost child can feel. My heart went out to her yet I was at a loss to make a satisfactory consoling gesture.

Comparing my depleted inventory and shameful background, I was convinced that I could never hope to be a fitting substitute for this gently nurtured boy. I wonder today if I had been able to assume a positive attitude whether my life would have been entirely different. This kind and endearing woman moved something deep within me. Still, the hard crust of my personality needed more time to remove its deficiencies.

Her kindness also consisted of bequeathing me her son's clothing. Among the items was a handsome overcoat, its expense undoubtedly a great sacrifice on her part, for she was a widow. Lovingly, she caressed the garment as she presented it to me. I had great difficulty in repressing my tears and deep feelings. This coat served me well for several years. Often I considered my unworthiness to be its recipient; as a good boy he met an early death while I, an almost hopeless miscreant, lived on.

During this time I had lost my job at the hospital as a result of a fight with another boy. I recall this incident vividly—a common adolescent conflict usually settled with words. I must confess that I easily resorted to physical force to express my resentments. Of the many jobs in my past, too numerous to mention, I have never felt a loss so keenly and for so long as this one. My attachment was profound for I found my stay here interesting and pleasant. Also, I felt a sense of guilt because this position was made possible by a person in the Smith household.

Shortly thereafter I found work in one of the large department stores in the Loop. This was a very pleasant situation with light duties and a tolerant supervisor. My routine included tracing complaints of customers, which allowed me access to all departments. The boring monotony of past work experiences existed not at all.

Here I met my first real girlfriend. Our social activities included the movies and picnics, often together with another couple. The amenities enjoyed in the process, seemingly so insignificant, were very important in adding a new attraction for me. While this relationship did not involve promiscuousness, necking added to its fascination. This pleasant creature I knew in my youth was effervescent in personality and comely in appearance. The shade on my past was in the process of being drawn, and I beheld the increasingly beautiful twilight. I had a room in a nice home, the privilege to go as I pleased, a satisfying position, and social interests that filled my cup to the brim.

After several months I felt that I deserved a raise in salary, however small the increase. My request was denied, and I foolishly quit out of what can only be described as a stubborn tantrum. Department stores are not prone to raise the salaries for clerical personnel and my duties did not involve any selling. Only much later was I able to realize and accept this fact. With particular fondness, I remember my superior's plea to remain. It was my good fortune to work under his always cordial and considerate supervision.

Trudging the streets in my quest for work, I found a clerical situation paying a fair salary. I continued night school as well. Eighteen months had now elapsed—the longest period without arrests or confinement since the age of six. I reached my nineteenth birthday that year.

My health gradually improved but I had a problem arising in the morning. It seemed I couldn't often report to work on time. Frequently late, usually only by a few minutes, I became the butt of my fellow workers' jibes. They referred to me as Rip Van Winkle. Eventually, however, I was discharged after repeated warnings for tardiness but never for fighting. In this respect at least, I was improving.

I lost the position as clerk because of my sleepy headedness, and in the next few months found employment part-time—usually for a few days at some department store or other miscellaneous odd job. The sporadic occasions of these temporary jobs did not provide the steady income to make ends meet. Consequently, I became about three months in arrears with my rent at Mrs. Smith's. She never pressed me, however. She was concerned by my quitting night school and expressed misgivings about marriage. She also cautioned me about the imprudence of my keeping late hours in which I had indulged during my courtship.

The matter of my debt to her concerned me deeply, since I knew she was needful of this income. I repaid her a short time after my marriage some several months later, which gave me an immense feeling of satisfaction. The memory of my negligence to this fine woman haunts me to this day. The mystery of destiny at times follows an inexorable pattern and often leaves in its wake an inexplicable debris and wounds that never quite heal. I shall always feel that I abandoned her in this storm.

5 Hold-Up at High Noon

Clifford R. Shaw married at this time and my life was further enriched by the welcome invitations that Hetta Shaw extended to me to visit their apartment near Jackson Park in a middle-class section of the city. The character of our relationship was not one that embraced merely professional interest in my past. Our conversations were casual and covered the usual topics of the day. Visits to the Institute for Juvenile Research allowed sufficient opportunity to deal with my story.

Our friendship became deep and sincere. These frequent interludes allowed me the privilege of borrowing some of his books that held an insatiable interest for me. An Irish barrister's admonition to me once "to seize the value of experience second hand" was being practiced. The wholesome influences were beginning to rub off and submerged any ideas of returning to the old associations that led to crime. The road ahead appeared promising and each step was taken eagerly and confidently.

Shaw many times encouraged me to become a salesman, a profession for which he thought I was especially suited in terms of ability and temperment. He obtained an opportunity for me to try my skill in this field and I found the work extremely fascinating. During my rounds of selling, I met the woman I was to marry, and the pattern of my adult life took shape.

My future wife and a brother were the breadwinners in a broken home that included her mother, bedridden with a chronic illness. There was warmth and cordiality in their welcome, and I found their accepting attitude extremely pleasing. Within this household were the apparent evidences of the brave struggle to somehow meet the challenge of economic conditions. The Victrola proudly displayed in the living room served to heighten our courtship. I became a member of their inner circle of friends, attended parties, and learned to dance. The intricacies of the foxtrot, waltz, and two-step were assiduously mastered in the months that followed. The intimacy of participation in this family gave me a distinct feeling of belonging.

The routine of this courtship also included church attendance, as she and her mother were devout in this respect. We went to services at the Moody Bible Church on the North Side and the exhortations of the minister found me responsive. We also attended some of the meetings of Aimee Semple McPherson, who was conducting a revival at the old Colliseum on Wabash Avenue. The dramatic effects of this experience on me were never lost, despite the ravages of future years that at times shook my faith.

My wife and I possessed an emotional desire and a physical hunger for each other. We were as two children, essentially confronting the same problems of life in our own way. Even in view of the disadvantages forced on us, we enjoyed the essence of our love.

Our marriage took place in the setting of the beauty of autumn, just a few days after I became twenty-one years of age. There could be no doubt as to my affection for my wife. Mindful of the poverty and misery of my childhood, it behooved me to shrink from entering into a union that most certainly would result in bringing children into the world. My present state of employment precluded my eligibility to assume the responsibility that this would entail. The urgency of our situation required a trust in Providence for some sort of a miracle to meet the challenge of the future.

Our marriage ended in divorce after a long separation. In truth, I must confess this came about owing largely more to my shortcomings than to hers; she tried hard to make the union work. This failure to a great extent can be attributed to several experiences due to the Great Depression. Having married at a rather early age and without a vocation commensurate with my responsibilities, I was fortunate in obtaining employment that thrust me into sales work. Some people, though few, are natural born salesmen. In my case, I was raw material of the first order, and my determination carried me past my deficiencies.

The onset of the depression began at the end of our first year of marriage and did not affect me until the epidemic of bank failures swept the country. I had risen to a manager status, with a probable potential of earning $10,000 per year, which at that particular time was fairly good money. Unfortunately, the price structure of the merchandise I was trying to sell, the piano, found a negative receptivity. What I offered was a distinct luxury that was beyond the capacity of consumers beset not only with the loss of bank savings but also jobs.

The ensuing several years found me floundering with a great measure of discontent, trying my hand at a few jobs that held no promise for my desired place as head of the household. My return to salesmanship was discouraged by the attitude of my wife who felt that a steady job was preferable to the uncertainties of sales work.

During this period I had many visits with Shaw and his family, which I enjoyed greatly. Continually, he apprised me of the importance of accepting things the way they were—to be satisfied with a nice family, and, above all, to do the right thing—all of this never in the role of the inquisitor, rather, in his inimitable, tolerant fashion. Many a weekend I spent on his farm, helping in my small way at various tasks. His chidren practically grew up with me, and of course Mrs. Shaw always proved gracious and hospitable. It certainly would not be far fetched to state that the Shaws were my real parents.

Fortuitously, I obtained employment as a salesman for a piano firm, with a small salary sufficient to meet the necessities of food and shelter and thus became a householder in the process. Quickly, our first child was on the way, and the problem of providing for his coming could only be solved by his birth in the City Hospital, since I had no funds. We lived in a furnished room, not lacking in hospitality from our landlord, an emigre from Germany who had served as a soldier in World War I. Through this association, I learned that these people were good and kind, refuting the concept of the Hun, so blaringly described by the media. What, indeed, a hypocrisy this was.

As a piano salesman, in the dead of winter on a crisp January morning in 1929, I was taken by my supervisor to canvass the Englewood District of Chicago. I was introduced to the gimmickry of pseudobargains, so prevalent in that period, designed to snare the unwary. The philosophy of the head guard at the House of Correction, that business was to a great extent a legal form of larceny, accurately reflected the piano trade.

On my second day in the field, however, after knocking on many doors, I was duly surprised by the rather abrupt appearance of a mother who declared it her mission to purchase a piano for her child. Quickly, I prompted her to tarry while I made arrangements for convenient transportation to the Loop. Arriving in a taxicab and consummating the deal, much to my credit, enabled me to stay and absorb the experience that was invaluable in my future sales career.

The advent of the electric radio upon the music scene presented the piano industry with a competitive threat and the popular acceptance of the phenomenon all but throttled the hitherto prominent status of the piano as a symbol of a way of life. The small, upright piano and, of course, being in the right place at the right time, served as a milestone in furthering my career in sales work. Exposed for several months to a piano market held spellbound by the miracle of the radio, I was forced to learn the aggressive sales approach.

Eventually I was discharged, a common occurrence on piano row, the few blocks on Wabash Avenue that contained all the principal piano firms. It was not uncommon for a discharged member to apply to the nearest company, usually being hired by a rival located a few doors away. Working a few weeks for the new company, I was found wanting and discharged again.

Clutching my pay slip, on the way upstairs to receive my salary, I encountered one of my colleagues from the first company. When he inquired of my destination, I replied that I was fired. Without a moment's hesitation, he hired me to assist him in the radio department. This transaction merely involved collecting my final check at one window and filling out my new application at another, with the usual salary arrangement. Placing radios on demonstration in homes was almost ludicrously easy and required very little persuasion on my part. Many householders would offer me a carte blanche invitation to take their piano gratis, simply to make room for the radio.

Examining my financial status, I found that my salary was paid against a very small commission, precluding any appreciable gain. As I had confidence in my ability, I contacted a jobber, requesting a recommendation to one of the dealers in reasonable proximity to my home. The dealer to whom I was sent was not prominent; still, he had an attractive store offering several lines of accepted brands and seemed well-stocked with merchandise. Explaining my desire to achieve top commission, an agreement was made, and I became an independent operator. I was apprehensive because I knew that in order to survive I must produce sales without the cushion of a salary or a drawing account. Striking out, I began canvassing the area nearest the store. The second day I was rewarded with a sale for my efforts, solidifying my faith in the process.

I experienced a banner month of sales for October 1929, earning well over $300 in that period—a grand sum in those days. We began a savings account, accumulating a modest sum. Early in 1930, the first of a series of bank failures took place and many plants discharged workers, which further complicated the situation.

Meanwhile, my wife grew restive of living in a furnished apartment. Of course this also meant buying furniture, and in reassessing our financial condition we decided to risk going into debt for this additional purchase. We found a beautiful bedroom apartment with all the modern conveniences in an almost brand new building located on a divided street that boasted a parkway. It was quite idyllic, altogether exciting, especially in allowing us to escape the confining quarters of the kitchenette with its typical in-a-door bed that always reminded me of opening a can of sardines.

We spent a happy interim in this little apartment. Its location just across the street from a high school with its broad recreational field afforded me participation in many softball games.

The early months of the year 1930 found me a believer in the myth that the recent stock market crash was merely incidental and that the economy would right itself in due course. Indeed, I had yet to feel its effect, since I had no difficulty in maintaining my source of income in the field. As the months unfolded, the incidence of bank failures increased and most people lost their life savings. In addition, plants and firms discharged workers, many having years of service to their credit. Families began doubling up in occupancy and rent, attempting to meet the severity of conditions that were appalling, to say the least.

My sales took a dramatic drop and I found resistance to my efforts undeniably justifiable. My inability to pay the rent fell on the deaf ears of my landlord, who insisted on his money. When I failed to produce it, he promptly served a five-day notice to move. In addition to this debacle, my employer could not assume responsibility for my salary, regardless of the volume generated by my sales group or myself. The furniture so recently purchased and so attractively arranged in this beautiful apartment was not fully paid for, and there was little assurance that it would be, since conditions economically were becoming increasingly chaotic. My contacts with clientele became a succession of endless tales of woe by family heads cut from their source of income and denied access to savings accounts at banks held in receivership.

My employer went bankrupt, and my house of dreams sadly dissolved. In my interest, Shaw and I had a series of conferences regarding my adjustment to the general situation. Herein lies the essence of how real and sincere his feelings were for my welfare, for he was instrumental in finding a position for me with a small but steady salary that held some promise for the future. It ended tragically, however, because my superior resorted to a fake burglary to cover his shortages.

I was both astounded and fearful when the plan was revealed to me, especially when I considered Shaw's recommendation. I became torn. The old code of not ratting combated the responsibility and loyalty I owed Shaw and my employer. I consulted with Shaw and relied on his judgment to solve the problem. Without hesitation, he decided to reveal the plot and pointed out the futility of concealing an act of crime that could only reflect on me. As a result, my superior was discharged.

Before long, because of economic conditions, I too lost my job. The loss of this position placed my family in a very precarious position. Whatever increment I managed to wrest through my efforts was swept away by the repossession of household goods purchased in good faith. The year 1931 found us wallowing in the filth and grime of a loathsome tenement flat in a deteriorating section of the city. My wife secured employment in her field, which left me with the task of attending to the varied needs of my two boys, hardly out of the infant stage.

Fortunately, however, my past experience of living with my half sister, when I often was left with the task of her children's care, held me in good stead, and I was willing to respond to the demands of my own children. Nevertheless, I was torn from within. I seethed with increasing frustration and hated having to cope with the surrounding sight of crawling vermin that held a more than formidable foothold in the aged and decrepit building that was our miserable home.

My wife's working found me unwilling to accept its full reality. I was at a loss as to how I could resume my desired role as provider for the family. In my frustration I sought the company of my gambling cronies. The fleeting effects of this escape route did nothing to offer promise for a constructive solution to our problems. In addition, to further aggravate my mental state, I began to question the validity of the system and the legitimacy of its dogma.

The wreckage of the economic structure had now become a way of life. Scores upon scores of previously successful companies failed and left in their wake a procession of millions of people made victims. President Hoover now became the central figure for the hope of the country, and it must be honestly evaluated that he was an able administrator. One must be mindful, too, of the debris that he was expected to sweep away in order to bring about stability and confidence, so shattered by the collapse of the stock market. Tragically, the blame for the holocaust that struck the very foundation of the once mighty new empire was wrongfully heaped on this man. Hoover was limited in his executive capacity and unable to bring the necessary reforms so ardently hoped for by the populace.

He presented to Congress the Reconstruction Finance Act—a splendid and sound basic approach for the alleviation of the problems. The states in turn set up the tax structure to finance the various relief programs. It behooves me to recall that the House and Senate were shamefully engaged in selfish manipulation and in many cases throttling proposed bills merely to promote the ends of the reactionary elements of the two bodies, which were well represented by both the Republican and Democratic parties.

As an individual equally affected by the depressive effects of this period, I found myself examining the situation in its true light, unbiased by any political affiliation, which left me with the sad realization that too many of us as constituents had neglected our reponsibility to elect able and dedicated talent to the machinery that so vitally determines our destinies.

The fall of 1931 was approaching and found me embittered and depressed, looking for solace and escape in my card games. Then the one terrible act of my adult life that I shall always regret took place.

In evaluating my situation, it was natural that I discuss the prospects with my cronies, among them being a young man my age who expressed strong and violent feelings against the establishment—his father having lost his savings in a bank that had been considered almost impregnable. He revealed to me one day a well-worn pistol, fully loaded, and suggested we strike out with it and put the heist on any place that might mean some ready money. That we lacked a preconceived strategy indicated the naiveté of two rank amateurs embarking on a mission destined to endanger not only our lives but also possibly the intended victims'.

The fateful day arrived. Finding myself in possession of the revolver, my coconspirator would serve as the lookout and I would make the decision as to the location; all this in broad daylight, on one of the main thoroughfares of the city. Near a busy intersection at about high noon, I finally decided on a rather spacious store, revealing the presence of one person, obviously the proprietor. With a supreme effort, I subjugated the inward fears and doubts, and strode inside, arriving at a rear counter, in back of which appeared a rather formidable figure of a man who requested how he could serve me.

I answered in kind by drawing the weapon from an inner pocket and ordering him into the back room. We faced each other at arms' length. At my command, he attempted to wrest the pistol from me. Stepping back finally, I began to shoot—not to hit him but to force him to capitulate to my demand that he retreat to the confines of the inner quarters, away from the possible view of street passersby.

After firing five of the six cartridges in a wild fashion, I realized that this determined man would resist my attempt to coerce him. However, with just one bullet in the chamber, I was left with the choice of firing it directly at him or fleeing. The alternatives overwhelmed me as I could not bring myself to shoot him. Instead, I surrendered my gun to him. Something in my mental processes at this vital moment suddenly made me aware of the enormity of my act, and I became conscience stricken and wilted in the grasp of my victim.

In a trice, the store was filled with people, attracted by the deafening noise, and I was held securely awaiting the arrival of the police. Quickly they escorted me to the nearby squad car, and we proceeded to the station lockup where I was booked and then placed into a cell. Before me were some jeering men, one of whom particularly expressed a desire to attack me. The big form of the Irish lockup keeper appeared, and he firmly advised this man to retreat, leaving me with my own muddled thoughts of the nightmare that had just occurred.

My wife came and I absorbed the tirade of her criticism, having by this time fully realized the repercussions of my act of folly on her and the children. Suddenly, tears of sorrow and sympathy came from within her and she held me close. In spite of the iron bars that separated us, she assured me of her assistance in every way.

The judge at the preliminary hearing bound me over to the grand jury for assault with a deadly weapon and held me in lieu of $5,000 bond. Then I was led to the van that delivered me to the confines of the new county jail. I took some solace from the comparative luxury of these new quarters where the cells were clean and offered the comfort of a real bed compared to the squalidness of the ancient gray monstrosity, the old jail. There was also the day room to which we were let out during the day and where various games of cards and checkers were in progress. And too, the meals were fairly palatable, all things considered.

Meanwhile, Shaw was contacted and provided me with an attorney who visited briefly and informed me that he would do what he could to help. My crime called for a penitentiary sentence, since it carried the indictment of assault to commit murder. I must say I never had an intention to do anything of the kind, and since I expressed no oral intimation of my intended mission, there could be no legal charge of robbery. Thus, I was saved the stigma of being charged with a felony, and through the able efforts of my attorney I was convicted of a misdemeanor and sentenced once again to the adjoining confines of the House of Correction for the duration of one year. I was then twenty-three years old.

6 The Depression Years

As usual I was placed in the old North Cell House and assigned to the tailor shop, where I was given the stint of sewing two prison-made shirts daily. At the end of a month, my wife was allowed to visit. It so happened that the guard at the front door remembered me as a trusty of six years before when he was in charge of the cell house in which I was quartered at the time. Since he needed a crew of long-term prisoners to assist in the onerous tasks of his station, including the operation of the telephone switchboard that served the institution, I was a likely candidate. Thus, I was transferred to his charge, and immediately assigned to the switchboard, as well as running the errands of a trusty. Of course this was a welcome blessing.

I must say that my mind was on my family and the months of confinement found me depressed and concerned about their welfare. My general health began to fail and incipient stomach ulcers made their presence known by a gnawing and insistent pain. At this time a new superintendent took charge of the institution. He seemed to be concerned generally in improving conditions, and he was to be found early and personally investigating every nook and cranny of the prison. His attention was given particularly to the kitchen, which had served abominable food for many years, and this resulted in some improvement.

I fainted one day and was sent to the hospital for observation, and after a few days released to my department. The wife of the superintendent, noting my anemic condition, was instrumental in getting me the privilege of eating in the officers' kitchen, which probably saved my life since I could have never survived a general diet that only aggravated my condition. Deeply grateful for this unusual consideration, I found a new strength to sustain the remaining months of my confinement and impatiently counted each day's passing.

Having access to the outer perimeter of the prison, I often was tempted to walk out on the street in freedom from my restrictive situation. This, however, was more than precluded by two factors that held me in check. One, I could never go back to my family and, two, a certain sense of responsiblility to the guard who made this position of trust a distinct privilege. All the while my very being was crying out for the freedom of movement so apparently accessible, yet the invisible chain of restraint held me fast. My wife, meanwhile, found employment in the firm of a wonderful family, which proved a boon at this critical time and lessened somewhat my anxiety as to the welfare of the family.

Eventually the day of my release arrived and I met my wife at a pre-arranged place in the Loop. Happily reunited, and after a bit of refreshment, we proceeded home to see once again the children I had been isolated from for the past year. Arriving at the quarters that represented our home, I was overcome with an amazed loathing at the sight of one of the worst tenements. Within our apartment was the shabbiest cast-off furniture, and the filthiest rug, encrusted with remnants of food. Of course, I realized that my absence contributed to this miserable environment and that the efforts of my wife were to be admired and appreciated. Nonetheless I was determined to do something about extricating ourselves from this hovel—or so I thought.

The bureaucratic machinery of the government was trying desperately to bring relief by creating a tax structure to provide a program for the incensing horde of indigents, many with large families. At this time it was coincidental that my friend Shaw lived nearby, and I often walked across Jackson Park to his apartment, finding the hospitality of this family much to my liking. Since many families and individuals were now applying to the county for relief, Shaw saw no reason why I should not avail myself of this privilege and strongly urged me to do so. With more than a resigned sigh, I agreed and journeyed to the headquarters to file an application. Each month we received certain basic foods, mostly of a cereal nature, and a grocery order to be filled on demand at any store accepting the form.

At odd intevals, a social worker assigned to our case would visit the home. I noted with no small degree of annoyance her arrogant fashion in making an inspection of every room without invitation and in making derogatory remarks regarding my inability to find work, implying that almost anyone could find a job. This angered me no end, and I vowed to get off the relief roles as soon as possible.

Again, I found some escape in my card playing in joints throughout the city, but with hope that I might find employment as a dealer, since the returns were more lucrative. I managed to get on as a poker dealer in the back room of the cigar store, which was next door to a bookie joint. I experienced a certain amount of jealousy and antagonism from some of our habitués who regarded my appearance as an intrusion. I found my position precarious indeed, and eventually lost my place to another.

To add to our woes, early one morning while we were asleep we became the victims of a fire that was started by my children playing with matches. We were lucky to escape serious injury since the tenement was a tinder box. Only the prompt arrival of the fire wagons saved us from certain death. Since we needed new living quarters, the relief agency provided us with a squalidly furnished apartment, even worse than what we had left in ruins.

Within this new building lived a little boy about the age of my oldest son. He was often left to his own resources by his mother, who seemed to

be involved in activities not exactly in keeping with her maternal responsibilities. One day as I morosely surveyed the landscape of the backyard
strewn with rubbish, I observed this boy bullying my son who, with his
easygoing nature, seemed to more than tolerate this mistreatment. Angered
at his sufferance of this affront, I yelled at him to retaliate. In but a moment
he managed to throw the offending boy to the ground and pummel him,
much to my delight. Later I suggested to him his responsibility to protect
himself as being of utmost importance if he expected to meet life in the
future.

My wife found a job in her field. On the basis of this good fortune we
found an apartment in a better section of the city, and we began the
reconstruction of our lives. Starting with a pitiful handful of belongings,
but nonetheless happy, the future held at least the hope of something better
than our recent nightmare. I was willing to assume the care of the children
even though I yearned for our respective roles to be reversed. I took some
satisfaction in my attempt to give parental care to my children, yet I felt embarrassed and sensitive to the imagined attitudes of the neighbors.

The good people that employed my wife during my incarceration had
been paying our milk bill for an indefinite period. They came to visit us in
the new apartment and seemed to note the improvement in our lot. I was
offered a job in their firm in the shipping department, which I accepted with
alacrity. Though this required employing someone to care for the children,
it still presented us with an augmented income that allowed us to buy new
furniture, and we began to live like real human beings again.

The year 1936 definitely indicated that the country would recover
economically. The pump priming of the federal government had its effect,
however adversely interpreted by the most conservative element. The productive ability of the laboring man had been compensated adequately to
allow purchasing power to be maintained. (Today, of course, we are ex-
periencing the swing of the pendulum in the other direction. Labor unions
are well organized and exerting tremendous pressure that leaves manage-
ment no alternative but to raise prices, and this contributes to a spiral of in-
flation that shall continue until these two forces recognize that the time for
moderation and cooperation really is at hand.)

Although seven years had elapsed since that October day, the debacle of
1929, evidence of the debris was still apparent. Now I found myself
attempting to reenter the field of sales, and I managed to succeed in but a
limited fashion. The ulcer condition was becoming progressively worse,
creating periods of enforced rest at home and thus impeding the aggressive
style so necessary to achieve top earnings that would allow my wife to quit
and assume her responsibilities full in the home.

The growing boys required her presence and vital attention to provide
them with the training essential to their healthy development, both physi-

cally and morally. Somehow we managed to give our offspring enough of the things in a small way that assured them of our love. They went to camp every summer, and I encouraged them in sports such as baseball, bowling, and boxing. For example, I purchased a set of boxing gloves and we enjoyed our regular sparring sessions in the narrow confines of our living room, often endangering the furniture in the process. We also went to our share of major league baseball games, always cheering somewhat vociferously for the home team. Sundays usually found us having dinner in some good restaurant featuring food of a particular nationality. Thus the boys learned early the relative merits of people of various tongues, and in their delight their healthy appetites suffered not a whit.

In retrospect, the eventual failure of our marriage must be traced to myself. As I recall these golden moments of our experiences together, they comprise the very essence of the wine of happiness. We were, in addition, blessed by a reasonable state of behavior from our children, unlike problems found commonly in many families. My fixation in early adult life regarding my goals and ambition perhaps detracted me from my full appreciation of these things and, as I see it today, I would not trade these precious moments for the highest degree of success in the commercial world.

I persuaded my wife to quit her job and allow me to assume the role of breadwinner just before the outbreak of the great war of 1939. One day a ward committeeman knocked on our door soliciting support in his campaign for the office of alderman. I was particularly impressed by his personal efforts at canvassing, this path usually being relegated to lesser luminaries in his organization. I also found within his personality an unusual quality of sincerity and integrity. He enlisted me as a precinct captain and I became involved in the group activities for the young of the ward.

Since he was a Republican, faced with the task of challenging the powerful Democratic party, swept into power with Roosevelt's tremendous popularity, I regarded it as an opportunity to express a protest against the corrupt elements of the party in power. The incumbent alderman of our ward was the most notorious example. I prevailed upon my mentor to allow me to organize a softball team, for I saw this as an ideal way to draw out numbers for the organization. We did not win too many games, yet we did succeed in making an impression on the opposing political group that there was still some life in the GOP.

The aldermanic election proved to be a heated contest. I worked like a beaver in my precinct and was pleased by the results as we carried by a mere seven votes. Nevertheless, it was a great victory for me since the preponderance of votes here was at least ten to one along party lines. The final result in the ward was a very narrow margin for the incumbent. Immediately the hue and cry for a recount was vigorously pursued by our candidate. Because the election machinery was dominated by the Democratic party, few of us expected any relief from this quarter. When the recount was finally completed, we lost by a trifle over two hundred votes. Licking our wounds, we became at least consoled by looking forward to the 1940 presidential and senatorial campaigns with a confidence that at least the vulnerability of the opposition had been made apparent.

It must be noted that my political activities required a certain amount of energy and time that naturally took a toll on me both emotionally and physically. Since my stomach condition was progressively becoming worse, it was reflected in my earning capacity. Examining my foray into the political arena, I knew I was not eligible to assume any position of great importance. Still, there held the promise of the reward of a more secure job given usually to precinct captains. I most certainly could have used a soft position as the periods of enforced rest were becoming more frequent.

I was selected as a delegate to the Young Republican Convention in Springfield, the capital, which I found interesting, especially as I was able to meet some of the members of the higher echelon that made up the state organization. Our delegation had a dissident member who had been a thorn in my side and who I knew to represent a splinter group within our organization. I was almost positive that he was a ringer to create havoc among us. He used his physical size to bully those who cringed before him. He infuriated me and his efforts to dominate me found me unresponsive in any way.

In our suite in the Mark Hopkins Hotel, the inevitable showdown occurred when we came to physical blows. A senator, who could not fail to hear the noise of the altercation, quietly intervened and suggested that we not oppose one another. Our convention was well attended and one could detect a surging spirit of determination among the young and vigorous group to divert their full energies to the task of defeating the party in power.

My strenuous efforts in the 1940 campaign left me drained of energy, with the gnawing hell of an ulcer growing incessantly dangerous. And too, the family larder was in great need of replenishment. My brother, who for years drove a taxi cab, became concerned over my condition, both physically and financially, and begged me to join him to make a steady if small income. Meanwhile my wife found a job, and I could scarcely blame her, for on the altar of politics I jeopardized the very welfare of the family.

Weary and in pain most of the time, I threw in the sponge as it were and applied for a license to operate a taxi. This required answering questions about my background. Technically, I was never convicted of a felony and, keeping this in mind, I filled out the application, knowing that in the process, which would take several months, the fingerprints taken by the licensing bureau would eventually produce my yellow sheet. Then there would be a showdown as to whether I was eligible to work or not. Meanwhile, I jockeyed my cab, finding the redeeming factor of independence at least to my liking, and with the combined earnings of my wife we were secure.

My stomach pains began to grow alarmingly worse. The powders and milk and cream of the diet I followed were losing their effect in moderating the protest within me. One spring morning in 1942, after a very painful night at work, I awaited a streetcar to take me home. Suddenly I was seized by cramps so violent that I hailed a cabby and instructed him to take me to the nearest hospital.

In the receiving room I was examined, more or less, by two interns who seemed to treat my complaint as a simple bellyache. After about an hour of this bantering, I suggested they take a blood count to determine whether I had an infection. Indeed, the results revealed an infection, as the white count was quite high. I was immediately taken to the operating room and no time was wasted by a surgeon, who was one of the finest on the staff. Awaking from the operation with tubes and needles inserted in various parts of my body, I was told I had suffered a perforation of the duodenum. The surgeon explained that the perforation was simply closed and that I must be on a diet and treatment in the future to forestall a recurrence.

When I finally came home, my wife encouraged me to rest as long as I needed to fully recuperate. I enjoyed being with my boys, preparing their food and caring for them. I realized the neglect that had resulted in the past from the absence of both of us while we worked. This was a critical marker in my marital life, for had I only submitted to a prolonged period of relative inactivity and dedicated myself to the duties of the household, everyone would have benefited.

However, after several weeks I grew restive and anxious to resume work. Pearl Harbor took place just prior to my operation. My draft status was settled at once by that board after viewing the incisions in my body, and I was literally chased out of the draft office. For some reason this disappointed me, since two of my older brothers had been veterans of World War I. I, too, wanted to be a part of the force to meet the challenge that threatened the free world. In spite of my history of being a delinquent and incipient criminal, I never once doubted our political system nor our country. I always viewed my father's immigration here as a blessing and heritage to me. Thus, my regret at being rejected was keen.

I resumed my taxi career and found business brisk, for there were many restrictions placed on the civilian, including gasoline consumption, resulting in a greater demand for our services. I followed the rules set down by my doctor regarding diet and tried to relax, appreciating his advice that nervous tension created ulcers.

During these war years, I found time to visit the Shaws at their farm. This association was a vital part of my life, and crystalized a deep and abiding affection for this family. Sadly, I began to note the aging of

Clifford Shaw. The mounting urgencies of his varied projects and a heart condition eventually led to a rather premature death. As I see it clearly now, he became at once the father to me that I never knew. He contributed to taming the wild nature within me, whatever the cause, and I incorporated into my present life much of what he represented.

7 Kankakee State Hospital

The middle years are often regarded as critical, and changes that take place affect our lives dramatically. My wife began to show signs of coolness and indifference toward me. She often gave indications that her role as bread-winner was of predominant significance. This, of course, is probably true, but it certainly did not placate my sensitive nature nor dent my fixed ideas about the importance of my role in this respect.

I began to note her almost total disregard in cooperating with the house-work, and hours she spent writing long letters to someone in the service. I made no comment, as I wished to fully evaluate this development. Quietly I viewed this with much concern and realized that the threat to the solidarity of the family was rearing its ugly head. Not knowing what she really wanted, but still noting the increasing coolness between us, I realized that there was another interest in her life that superseded our past relationship. Ordinarily, if not for the children, I would have left without a moment's hesitation, for I always believed in not being where I was not wanted, and this included mar-riage. However, I was haunted by the thought of my boys being dominated by another father. My own stepmother was so cruel and brutal toward me that it led me to attempt a reconcilation of our apparent estrangement.

I calculated that the interest in someone probably existed where she worked, and if I could prevail upon her to quit we might keep our marriage together, if only for the sake of the children. I presented her with an ultimatum of either resigning or my leaving. I could not tolerate her total in-difference to my feelings regarding her behavior. She refused point blank and used an excuse that the war effort demanded her continuing the posi-tion she held. In the heated discussion that followed, I asked who was to be eligible to fight the next war. To this there was no answer, and at this mo-ment I realized that the end of our union was inevitable.

I took my few belongings and obtained lodging in a hotel, finding meanwhile some solace in embracing John Barleycorn, which in the past never led me to a habit of imbibing. Upon reassessing the dilemma, I de-cided to make one more attempt at a possible reconciliation. Holding our rendezvous in the home, we became involved in a most heated discussion. It so happened that a table knife was lying on the dining room table where we were seated. I idly fingered it, with absolutely no thought of using it as a weapon. Bear in mind that I could have subdued her quite easily with but one blow. There actually was no need for me to use a weapon to attack her.

In a moment of bitter frustration, I left the apartment through the kitchen entrance, not realizing I had on no shoes. Since it was the month of August, I really did not realize this missing part of my apparel. Eventually I was picked up by the police as I trudged the street. There is no question that I was suffering from a temporary blackout, and when I regained my normal equilibrium I found myself in a psychopathic hospital.

This was a terrible, traumatic experience to me, since my presence here indicated that I was insane. I called the nurse, attempting to tell her that I was fully recovered and wished to be released. This was met by a harsh command to be quiet. Shortly thereafter I was herded into a courtroom and summarily committed to a state hospital, without any questions asked or answers given. Having been transported to various other institutions in the past, I never experienced such fear and foreboding as in this journey to a kind of confinement, totally alien to any I had known before.

I startlingly realized that my rights as a person were being impounded and that there was no window of relief for the future. On the bus through the beautiful and scenic countryside I began formulating my ideas as to how I could extricate myself from this predicament. I knew that I would have to display my sanity to the satisfaction of the authorities. I determined to create this impression and conduct myself accordingly.

We were all taken to the diagnostic quarters, quite modern in every respect in contrast to the many old and decrepit buildings of the institution that housed a few thousand other patients. Bearing in mind that my behavior was being closely observed, I took great care not to display emotional outbursts of any kind and hoped that I would be released shortly. The screening process in this diagnostic ward involved interviews and tests designed to pinpoint the phobias and aberrations of each patient. In spite of my awareness of the precariousness of my position, I exposed myself to the mercies of the staff doctors whose evaluations had a great influence on the destinies of the patients in terms of the kind and length of their confinement.

In the dormitory of the diagnostic ward, which was very attractive, I joined the other patients in making the beds and vied with them to smooth every wrinkle in every spread. Suddenly one day, a patient working with me disagreed with another member of our group and began beating him. Since the aggressor was altogether a young man, I impulsively felt it unfair and rushed to the assistance of the victim. In subduing the aggressor, I was surrounded by several other patients and an attendant who held me in abeyance. Summarily, I was sent to the hydrotherapy ward, reserved for rule breakers and the most violent cases.

If one were to direct a typical horror movie, the scene of this barred enclosure would present a weirdness that would exceed any eerie effect desired. I was frightened thoroughly by a score of the worst examples of maniacal personalities who were beset with obsessions accompanied by wild and incoherent shrieking. The paint on the walls was peeling and the bare fixtures served to accentuate the inhospitality of this dungeon. The attendant allowed me to stand for a moment before he assigned me to a cubicle. As I lay upon a cot, I contemplated my situation with the greatest fear of my life. I began to see myself held forever in bondage, restricted to the constant association of blubbering idiots and psychotics.

After a few days, during which I took stock of the general routine of the ward, I decided to offer my services for assisting in any way, sweeping the floor or aiding the attendants. Gruffly, an attendant handed me a broom and instructed me to sweep the floor. In taking it, I opened the door to my release from this vile place if not my ultimate salvation. In a very short time I was assisting them in their various duties such as packing patients in hot and cold packs and restraining violent individuals.

After a few weeks I was transferred to a ward that was a dumping ground for those considered violent. Overcrowded and shabby would be paying the appearance of this ward a compliment. It was considered the Alcatraz of wards—the point of no return. Shortly after arriving, the attendant's wife took notice of me. In a few weeks I was assigned to their kitchen and helped to serve their meals. I acquired a share in their fare, which was a privilege I appreciated.

The routine in this ward was monotonous, with only a weekly movie and a daily walk. There was very little entertainment in the ward dayroom. Some of the reasonably coherent patients played cards and checkers. The rest existed in isolation with their thoughts, and stared into space. My objective was to be transferred to a working ward, a stepping stone to freedom. I begged my brother and my wife, while visiting me, to have me transferred. I noted one repetitive theme during her infrequent visits—I want to see you well. I could never be released without her consent.

Having access to the outside of the ward in my duties, carrying in supplies and taking out the garbage, I easily could have dashed for my freedom. Again, I was prevented by my sense of loyalty to the kind couple who trusted me. Also, I wanted to be released properly—to be legally with my wife and children.

Finally, my brother persuaded the staff doctors to reassign me to a work ward and I gained a relative measure of freedom. I assumed the duties of assisting the cook in the big kitchen that provided the dietary needs of the patients. Now that I was in a position to demonstrate my fitness for release, I began to put pressure on my wife to sign the necessary papers. Her complaint virtually tied the hands of the administration because the chance always remained that I might do her bodily harm or possibly kill her. In quite a few cases in the past, this had actually happened and the authorities, therefore, were loathe to let me go.

After a couple of months in the work ward, I came to the conclusion that I must take things in my own hands and walk off the grounds. I continued to receive the same ambiguous reaction from the woman I married who professed great love for me but would not do the one simple thing to provide for my release. One night I simply walked away from a dance in the auditorium and boarded a bus to Chicago.

On the road I had time to evaluate the many stories brought back by escapees. I knew the pattern to avoid. Patients returned to the scene of their troubles and were picked up and sent back to the house of horrors. Bearing this in mind, I found a job in a nightclub washing dishes. No application was necessary, and I found a simple room away from the common beat and was as obscure as possible.

As a dishwasher, I was in a position to observe the ministrations of the service bartender whose station was close to mine. I became fascinated by his expert manipulation in concocting mixed drinks, and it occurred to me to learn the profession. Many bits of conversation were the start of a simple friendship. When I broached my wish to learn his art, he was quick to cooperate. He began with a demonstration of the various glasses and gave me the recipes for the common drinks. He explained that I would learn the others as I went along. I desired a job that would qualify me to present myself to either my wife or the authorities with clean hands and regain my legal status.

My bartender friend allowed me to assume his place at times. Under his critical attention, I gradually became dexterous and reasonably accurate in filling orders, some of which came with the rapidity of a machine gun. He pronounced me capable and urged me to leave the dishes for the more gentle art of glasses. Since it was wartime and jobs were going begging, it became easy to find one as a service bartender in a large restaurant.

The following can be considered reasonably accurate, but I have been able to piece it together only by conjecture. I must have contacted my wife and we resumed some sort of relationship. In this period I required hospitalization for what she said was a recurrence of my troubles. She engaged the services of a psychiatrist who gave me a series of electric shock treatments.[1] Released from this hospital, I discovered that my memory of recent events was absolutely blocked out. What is more, my memory of this episode never returned.

I found lodging at a hotel. Somewhat in a daze, but nevertheless aware of my responsibility to make a living, I applied for a selling job. At this particular time, the atomic bombing of Japan and the war's end occurred. Of this, of course, I obtained knowledge second hand.

Note

1. In a subsequent interview Stanley clarified this incident.

Jon. About these shock treatments, let me see if I understand. The Psychopathic Hospital was a short stay and then you were sent to the State Hospital?

Stanley. I was only at the Psychopathic Hospital two days.

J. You're not talking about shock treatment taking place at the State Hospital?

S. No, there was none there. This happened at a private hospital after my escape. My wife took me—I don't know how in the hell she did it—it's all blacked out over a period of six to eight months. These shock treatments did it. Now this sonofabitch that did it, she might have steered me into the hospital on some other pretext, and they gave me the works.

J. Do you remember what happened before you went to that hospital?

S. I don't know. You see, my memory is burned-out before and after it happened.

8 Life on the Hydrotherapy Ward

The skein that forms patterns in our lives takes peculiar turns, and changes often emanate from comparatively trivial incidents. One of my sales was to a part owner of a bookie joint I had frequented in the past. I also knew him through pinochle sessions in which we struck up a warm and convivial friendship. He was in charge of the regular weekend poker games.

Knowing of the fabulous wages of poker dealers, which included tokens known commonly as tips, I explained my desperate situation and asked him for an opportunity to deal in his game. He gave me a chance that weekend, and I was the happy recipient of a financial return that more than secured my maintenance. I had the rest of the week free, which gave me an excellent opportunity to recuperate from the shock treatments.

I continued contact with my wife, but strictly on my own home ground, as I was in deadly fear of going to her home and risking an incident that would send me back to the asylum. I knew that she was not to be trusted, especially after I demonstrated my sanity at the hospital and she continued to refuse to sign the papers for my release. This boggled my mind no end, for in our meetings she expressed great affection for me. This placed me at a crossroad mentally, much like the man on the trapeze. At intervals she brought the boys to my general area for dinner and other recreation. I confess that I gave her very little in the form of support, mainly because I had all I could do to take care of my own needs. I do remember, however, buying the boys a complete wardrobe. They were in high school at this time and it gave me a measure of satisfaction.

A nearby dance ballroom found me a constant patron and afforded me an opportunity to become acquainted with various women who contributed to my sense of well-being. An account of my associations in the gambling fraternity is also in order. Cooperation and understanding in time of need distinguishes this group. In daily relationships they lacked hypocrisy and called a spade a spade. This interim was vitally important in assisting me to overcome the traumatic experience of being incarcerated in a mental hospital. I shall always recall with deep appreciation those who sympathized and accepted me within their circle.

In a twinkling, my holiday from concern about making a living ended as a result of a clamp down on all gambling in the city. This was permanent, not the ordering of a few days' freeze so often practiced in the past. I applied for my old taxi job again. I went through the contortions of applying for a license, knowing that in a few months the yellow sheet would come back to haunt me. Nevertheless, I looked forward to a period of working until the axe fell. And I accumulated a savings fund against that fateful day.

The hotel in which I lived was located a short distance from Lake Shore Drive. Though relatively small, it was exceptionally clean and well managed. It was always a welcome haven. The manager, George, and I became good friends and over the years, whenever I was arrears in my rent, he carried me until the wheels of fortune turned favorably. I was always able to win a hand in a card game and I was becoming more proficient in this skill.

The day arrived when my garage man informed me that my license was revoked. Learning that the lunchroom just across the street where the drivers congregated was for sale, I became interested in purchasing it. Because the small sum I had saved was not enough, I confided to my wife my desire to go into the restaurant business. Comparing our financial resources, we arrived at the conclusion that we could just manage to pool the small sum required to make the transaction. There was too much to be done to transform this place. I visualized the improvements and a menu that would attract customers. The first few weeks took up much of my energy.

My quarters at the hotel were close by. One night I was awakened by a loud rap at my door, and low and behold there was the form of a policeman, who summarily ordered me to dress. Ignoring my questions as to why I was being arrested, he gruffly told me to quickly comply with his command. I was taken to the psychopathic hospital in a patrol wagon. There my protests fell on deaf ears, and after the usual details of reception I was ordered to a bed and told to remain quiet.

Soon I was transported back to the state hospital. There was no hearing of any kind. I was shocked and confused as to why this happened—there was no reason for this seizure. No time was wasted in placing me in the hydro ward. Since my yellow sheet had numerous items that suggested episodes of violence, I could easily be classified as at least a potential criminal personality, and thus be transferred to another institution reserved for the criminally insane. From the information I had gleaned, the chances of one's release from this institution were slim indeed.

Resuming my cooperative attitude with the attendants in this snake pit, I had no trouble in gaining their confidence. No one could understand why I was sent back. They were aware that someone was instrumental in filing a complaint against me. Since I had not removed the stain of my previous commitment by regaining my legal rights, I was in effect persona non grata in the eyes of the law and subject to confinement at any time. I had myself to blame, for I had exposed myself by resuming the relationship with my wife.

On the ward was a young and rather intelligent fellow, quite rational and engaging in personality, and we struck up a friendship. He had a marital problem quite similar to mine in that his wife was carrying on an affair with another man. It was apparent that Bill was blocking the traffic as it were, and she found it expedient to have him committed. Comtemplating this in sympathy, I realized that the practice of putting people out of circulation could be accomplished by anyone so inclined, since the court procedure left little recourse to an institutionalized person.

My attendant strongly advised me to write to my wife, to request her to visit. Almost unbearable resentment toward her existed ever since I was seized so unceremoniously. I was firmly convinced that our relationship had reached the final breaking point, for in reality she was not in any sense justified in having me confined. My perplexity regarding this left me with the conclusion that the love we once knew had turned into hatred, whatever the reason might be on her part. An answer to my letter was received eventually, and the gist was a rather ambiguous line of reasoning that she wanted to see me well. Also, she promised to see me.

I assumed my duties in assisting the attendants. I hoped that Bill, of whom I grew fond, would join me in my front-choice quarters. We secretly plotted that objective and I coached him to ingratiate himself with the attendants and follow my strategy of cooperation. Squelching his animosity against all the forces that sequestered him in chains of bondage, he emerged from his hostile attitude and emulated the course I found so successful in gaining an advantage over the routine of this closely guarded violent ward.

The general treatment of the patients must be mentioned briefly. It is quite true that a certain amount of brutality was inflicted upon some of the patients. However, in all fairness, I must say that in most instances there existed some justification for this, inasmuch as the violent nature of a number of the patients obsessed with delusions and hallucinations required a firm not gentle approach. Generally, though, there was a sort of spirit of passive compassion by the attending staff. This compared favorably with the almost total disregard by the doctors.

Eventually, Bill joined me up in front, grateful for this privilege. Next our objective was to obtain a staff hearing concerning our release. We began a quiet campaign to gain attention from the doctors who passed through the ward on their rounds.

Finally the day arrived when one of the doctors responded with a promise to arrange a staff hearing for both Bill and me. Jubilantly, we awaited the day of the hearing, feeling that we could each state our case and gain our release. So similar were our histories that we would both receive a favorable response from this body, composed of more than a score of people. In due time the hearing was held.

After Bill's case was heard behind closed doors, I was called. Before me appeared a group of serious-minded men, and I wondered how I could possibly convince them of my eligibility to resume a normal life. I had determined beforehand to confine my remarks to their queries as nearly precisely and briefly as possible, thus avoiding any rambling that might be construed as abnormal. Asked to be seated on a raised podium, the questioning began by the assistant superintendent, a rather feisty and arrogant personality. Included in his approach was a general breakdown of my past life in various institutions. Also, he brought up questions regarding the book I wrote with Shaw.

Divining his strategy of arousing my emotions, I resisted my anger and answered his inquisitions with a degree of equanimity that apparently frustrated him, and he brutally shot shaft after shaft—with a barrage of questions that mainly had to do with my delinquencies and acts of crime. Seething with indignation, the desire was strong within me to seize this vile and contemptible persons posing as a doctor. However, he ran out of breath momentarily, and I took this opportunity to ask the staff if I could say something on my behalf. As they acceded to my request, I began by asking how a state of normality could be described and told them that I was at a total loss as to why I was seized and confined against my will without my constitutional rights for a hearing. The answer was a complete wall of silence.

Shortly, the hearing was terminated and I was led out to the attendant who brought me. He congratulated me on my deportment and commented delightfully on my queries of the board. There exists a certain vein of alienation between doctors and attendants based on the burden of work that falls on the latter, who are also underpaid. It can be assumed that most of the staff doctors merely regard their tenure as a necessary step to a private practice that will yield a lucrative livelihood, as a result of the prestigious experience in a state hospital.

After a brief interim, Bill and I received the same stereotyped and quite sterile note from the superintendent. Incidentially, he was a typically pompous sort of individual, devoid of compassion for any of the unfortunate wards under his care. The note merely stated that our release was not to take place at this time. This bombshell left us in deep shock. Sadly, we realized that we would be forced to violate the confidence of the head attendant by escaping.

The attendants were perplexed by the results, and I am sure that if they had the authority, we would have long since been on our way to freedom. Bill revealed his possession of a bit of a hacksaw blade about a half-inch in length, hardly sufficient for severing the bar that would let us out. However, I began to try to make an indentation, discovering with considerable time and painstaking effort, that success was possible.

One morning a passing attendant threw an object on the bed, and we were met with the sight of a full-sized hacksaw blade. Bill could not believe it, and in truth I rubbed my eyes to be certain I was not dreaming. Carefully we stowed this important tool out of sight and began preparation for filching the necessary clothing, including shoes, all of which were forbidden to us, except pajamas.

The institution was well settled and the bar almost severed by a late hour. We snapped it off, squirmed our way out, and leaped to the ground. Our run across the ground to the outer ridge met with no encounter. We entered the town, avoiding main intersections and found our way to the outskirts. I cautioned Bill about main highways and we made our way across fields that represented the farmlands of the area.

9 Going West

As dawn began its silvery intrusion, we spotted a long row of high hedges in the distance. I led Bill to them, and in exhaustion we sank to the ground. Prudently, we decided to remain under the protective shadow of the hedges throughout the day. When darkness came we resumed our flight across meadows and fields, some with ground freshly broken by spring plowing. Arriving at a farmhouse with its share of outbuildings, we entered a large barn. We rested in its inviting store of abundant hay. Our exhaustion was made worse by our limited endurance.

After a bit of relaxation, a welcome interlude, Bill and I toured the farm buildings, seeking additional clothing to supplement the meager raiment with which we fled; scarcely enough to warm our bodies in the sharp, biting climate of an early spring morning. Suddenly, Bill called me to his side. He had discovered an automobile stored in the barn and pointed to a large set of keys in the ignition. We lost no time in deciding to appropriate the vehicle and quickly make our way to the city and its anonymity.

We peered out of the farmhouse for any sign that we were discovered poaching. The motor started without delay. We found the main highway to Chicago without incident and in an hour were in the protective haven of the city. Discussing our strategy for the future, Bill wanted to continue using the car. This I vetoed immediately, as it presented certain arrest if approached by some roving policeman in a squad car.

Each of us had several dollars that we carefully had saved from the bounty of visitors and the small contributions of attendants for small services. Thus we had the means for safe transportation out of the jurisdiction of the state. Bill had a sister to go to, and I decided to board the first bus to St. Louis just across the border. Vowing to keep in touch, we parted and resumed the freedom we once knew and shared so deeply.

I sat impatiently in the bus waiting for its departure. Examining my pitiful worldly possessions of the moment, I found the sum of nineteen cents, a deck of cards, pocket comb, and handkerchief. As the bus approached the outskirts of the city, I marveled at my good fortune in escaping the hellish confinement of the past. Dawn was breaking as I alighted in Missouri, outside the state that insisted on labeling me a maniac.

Upon self-examination, there is no question that I must confess to moments of abberation and emotional outbursts that may resemble the manifestations of one demented. I have often observed these qualities in others considered fairly normal. The ambiguity in the determination of the normal mind by qualified and trained individuals leaves much to be desired. The fate of too many unfortunates is decided by politically appointed judges who are unqualified to pass judgment on alleged mental illness. One of the greatest indictments against society consists in allowing almost any person, often even a relative, to file a complaint against an individual. Our antiquated judicial machinery needs special refurbishing regarding the commitment of a person to a mental institution. Too many are confined wrongfully.

As I walked the sidewalks of St. Louis that spring morning, debating whether to spend the remainder of my bankroll on a cup of coffee, my eye caught sight of a number of coins strewn before me, probably thrown by some inebriated person in the night. Staring with glee at this bonanza, I retrieved the sum of ninety cents which, together with my nineteen cents, allowed me to have a good breakfast and plan some effort to gain employment.

On the riverfront stood a large and rundown restaurant where I ordered coffee and a biscuit, conserving my newfound wealth for perhaps another meal. When I inquired of the proprietor about employment, he asked if I would wash dishes and do the porter work. Not bothering to ask about wages, I accepted with a deep feeling of gratitude. The next few weeks I worked diligently at the onerous tasks demanded of me, not minding one bit, for before me I saw the future opening up. I saved every penny not required for living expenses, with the thought of going west to California to make a start there.

I noticed one day a number of commissary labor offices offering work on the railroad as track laborers, often referred to in the vernacular as *Gandy Dancers.* Having saved over $20, I decided to ship out on one of these gaffs, hoping to go as far west as possible. The number of others accompanying me were considerable and filled several large coaches.

Seated next to me was a handsome young man with blond hair that accentuated unusually attractive features. Looking down, I discovered that he was without shoes. He explained ruefully that he was an alcoholic, in which, of course, he was not alone as almost all the passengers were in this category. Someone had stolen his shoes while he was on a binge, he explained. We discovered our destination to be a small town in central Iowa, not much of a distance in the west, to be sure, but I really did not care. I wanted to crawl further into a world of anonymity. Any avenue away from the state hospital suited me fine.

We reached the camp that would house us and found our quarters consisting of the barest necessities, a bunk and not much more. I began my task working on the roadbed with the gang, swinging a sledge hammer. Using it was a real challenge in my condition, and I did not expect to last very long.

A few days later, a three-day holiday gave us an opportunity to dwell on our lot. As for myself, I decided to chuck the job.

My fair-haired companion, a native of South Carolina, and I formed a trio and boarded an outgoing freight, not knowing its destination. It happened to be one of those slow, short-haul deals, and at the end of an intermittent journey we arrived in a fair-sized town. Since I had $20 in cash, and the nearest big city was Omaha, Nebraska, I decided to take the bus. Feeling sympathy for my companions, who could not yet pay their own way, I decided to compromise and furnish the fare for one of them. We tossed a coin and the choice fell to the individual from the South. Leaving my blond friend behind gave me a twinge of regret, but I just could not finance three tickets.

In Omaha I rented a room to enable us to get some much-needed rest. My few belongings were packed in a small duffle bag that contained a shirt, socks, underwear, and a cash balance of less than $10. Awakening from a deep sleep, I discovered my companion and my bag gone. Of course I was concerned, but I also realized that my erstwhile buddy was in need and that the temptation to filch my things was irresistible. In the past I had been guilty of doing the same thing. I concluded that a compensatory law seemed to have been in operation.

I left my room and sought the haven of the Salvation Army mission to obtain some assistance. Among the indigent and also the migrant, it had become knowledge that this agency can be depended upon in emergencies and is highly regarded. Standing in front of the headquarters after being given temporary assistance, I caught sight of my blond friend and shouted to him. He informed me of the good fortune to be picked up hitchhiking by a good samaritan who fed and clothed him, brought him to Omaha, and gave him a bit of money.

He had a room and asked me to join him. I remarked that the tossing of coins had excluded him, and I cursed this as a foolish whim on my part. Assuring me that he held this not against me, he also pointed out that his good fortune came as a result of it. He gave me a few dollars for pocket money and declared his intention to find an opening as a bartender, which was his trade. He had no trouble finding work at a leading hotel on Douglas Street, while I found a haven in several small clubs that ran card games with a small limit.

My friend Johnny, finding his job a boon, suggested that I try to get on and advised me to see the head bartender, commenting that I might at least get on as an extra for parties or conventions. I followed his advice and sought an interview with the head bartender, who surprisingly was quite young and of nice disposition. However, he regretfully told me that he did not have an opening at that time. Disappointedly turning away, I had almost reached the exit when he called me back. He told me he could use me as an extra for a few days for a number of parties. This work involved the simple pouring of whiskey and of course was quite easy for me. In addition, there was a continuation of about three weeks' work, which pleased me no end.

Eventually, I was given a steady job in the big room with Johnny. Pooling our talents, we served the most discriminate clientele who found our bar one of the best in town. The training that I received on Rush Street in Chicago in the intricacies of the art of a mixologist were of invaluable benefit to me, although I must say that Johnny was better by far. In addition, he had a handsome appearance that enhanced his style considerably.

But alas, poor Johnny could not resist the temtation to imbibe at the bar surreptitiously. I noticed this and prevailed on him to cease this practice, as I knew it meant instant dismissal. The supervision was constantly on the alert for all contingencies, and Johnny was caught and terminated. With all of his charm, talent, and ability, he followed the typical pattern of the confirmed alcoholic to its sad conclusion. Eventually he left town and I never heard from him again.

The manager of the hotel asked me to take charge and I was accepted fully as qualified and efficient, which contributed to my sense of self-esteem. The city I had known some twenty-five years before as a migrant boy had changed from a border town to a respectable metropolis. Its former myriad of ramshackle buildings were either razed or replaced by modern structures. The center of the city, close to my residence and job, contained a number of card clubs that also accepted wagers and disseminated results of various sporting events. An avid habitué in my element, I established associations that rounded out my routine of everyday living.

Safe outside the jurisdiction of the state from which I escaped, I decided to write to my wife. I did not in the least care for her personally because I greatly resented her role of prosecutor in my unwarranted confinement in the state hospital. But my boys were in her care, and I was anxious to know about their health and welfare. I assumed a diplomatic approach. I was surprised at her apparent friendly response to my letter and fascinated by this sudden change in her attitude. I accepted it gratefully though, for at least I could be kept informed about the boys. She came to visit me occasionally during the almost two years of my stay in Omaha, but I was wary about cementing our broken relationship.

In Omaha I found a measure of contentment through association with some of the best call girls, two of whom grew attached to me and would have appreciated a more permanent arrangement, which was precluded by my marital situation. I savored these rather intimate experiences for I discovered among the girls, and also the madams who controlled the hotel that found me its tenant, a warmth of acceptance that actually regarded me as a member of the family. Yet I wish to emphasize that I at no time shared in the proceeds of the income of its inmates, as I maintained my job as a bartender and paid my rent.

Since I was a tenant in this hotel, I became friendly with one woman, and what at the start was a business assignment became an intimate and free relationship. From the outset of our association, when she first entered my room and dropped her negligee to reveal one of the most beautiful and symmetrical human forms I had ever witnessed, she restrained her professional practice in order to be with me. We confided our respective backgrounds and grew quite fond of each other. At that time, and even today over twenty-five years later, I would not hesitate to embrace this beautiful creature as my own, in spite of her background. We took long walks, shopped, attended sporting events, and ate innumerable meals together. She contributed to what I look upon today as one of the happiest periods of my life.

My blissful routine was interrupted suddenly by being summarily discharged from my job that had propelled me to being in charge of all the bars in the hotel. In reporting for duty one morning, my time card was not in the rack and the timekeeper instructed me to see the cashier for my check. Confused and seeking some explanation, I found the manager, who was new, and was given no explanation except that I was dismissed. Leaving the premises, I vowed never to serve another drink as a bartender. Determined that my future would require an independence of the forces that might endanger my pursuit of a livelihood, I decided to reenter the sales field.

I answered an advertisement that requested help in converting gas stoves in the city of Milwaukee, Wisconsin, to accommodate a new mixture. I was hired at a rather handsome salary plus living expenses. Regretfully, I informed my love of my coming departure. She concealed her true feelings, but I could detect her sorrow, which was more than matched by by own. Bright eyed, she bid me goodbye. Promising to keep in touch, I boarded the train and vowed to myself to return to her at any cost. Little did I know that our paths would never meet again. I look back to this quite happy association with more than ordinary nostalgia, regretting greatly its ending.

I was never endowed with mechanical aptitude, and so I entered my duties in Milwaukee with a certain amount of trepidation. I was able to somehow stagger through the various problems that confronted me until one day I was faced with a complicated stove that defied my attempts to service it. I made an effort, only to be surrounded by an alarming heap of parts that I knew could never be reassembled. Spending far more time that ordinarily allowed for one call, I was visited by my foreman, a very nice person, who viewed the debris and my obvious inability to cope with the problem. Gently, he called me aside and suggested I resign. I heartily agreed to his request since I saved some several hundred dollars. Milwaukee was only ninety miles from Chicago.

10 Back to Chicago

Returning to my old hotel and good old George, the manager who received me like a prodigal son, I revived my previous life and enjoyed the resumption of past associations. I found a few temporary jobs that led me back to my calling as a salesman. I called my old supervisor and in the course of the conversation he explained that he was answering the advertisement of a music school. We met there. We were given an opportunity to sell enrollments for music lessons. For some reason I became intrigued with the offer, and since I had a week's wages to gamble, I started on this venture with enthusiasm.

Our sales manager was out of town the day I started, and the training program was assigned to an underling who accompanied me on but a single interview that consisted of only a few words. He then turned me out to fend for myself. For two weeks I strived, finding much receptivity, but not one single sale. Finally, after depleting my finances, but not my interest, I decided to turn in my paraphernalia and find another job. Providentially, arriving at the school, I was informed that the sales manager had returned and would like an interview with me.

In all outward appearances, the manager was the typical enthusiastic salesman thoroughly sold on his product. He proposed the idea to take me with him that night to show me his technique. His first call, in which I closely observed his closing technique, resulted in a sale and he put my name on the order. That I was pleased goes without saying, and I knew why I had failed in my efforts previously. He succeeded in another order on the next call, and I left him, wild again in high hopes for my future effort the following day.

I achieved a total of four orders my first day and a total of ten for the next week. Returning a handsome commission was in itself only a small part of my jubilation. The greater factor was the knowledge that I was capable in my given profession, and free of the encumbrance of supervision in menial jobs. Humbly, I acknowledge intervention of the man upstairs—had I left that school without success, losing confidence in myself—I perhaps would have never entered sales work again.

I worked at the school for the next five years, being consistently successful and, too, developing a fine friendship with my sales manager who was an equal partner in the ownership of a chain of schools. I became a constant visitor at his home, partaking of his lavish hospitality over and over again. My activities were punctuated with bouts of stomach attacks that rendered me impotent and seemed to grow more severe more often. Because of the highly profitable returns and the mastery of my presentations, the intervals I was able to work gave me enough income to sustain my needs. Meanwhile, my wife and I continued our association but always on my home ground. Now the boys were young men and my concern for them was eased somewhat.

At this time my sales manager requested me to accept an innovation in our financial arrangement that put me at a disadvantage. Against my protests, he obtained provisional approval from me, and assured me of a satisfactory adjustment in the future. Since our friendship was strong, I accepted his word. In following his new idea I discovered I could produce twice the ordinary volume of business but made less money in the process. Later he, too, found it impractical and discontinued the practice.

Now herein lies the crux of my character regarding others and their impact on my life. When the behavior of others affects me personally I have a rigid code of my own; I simply do not allow anyone to take advantage of me, and there is no compromise. My attitude is such that any violation of my welfare in any way is resisted at the slightest provocation.

After waiting respectfully for several months for an adjustment, the sales manager protested that he made no profit on this change and expected me to take my losses without question. Quietly informing him of his promise of reimbursement, he merely laughed. He did not realize how sensitive I was and, if it were not for our friendship, I could have ignored it quite easily. However, this involved a principle, and I decided to quietly sever our relationship. I made arrangements to join a rival firm but reserved my decision to inform him. Actually, I felt that he took advantage of me, and although I could overlook the present incident, I feared further acts of infidelity regarding our association.

I had maintained a correspondence for several years with Bill, my fellow escapee from the state hospital. He was a dedicated friend, who actually carried out a program to purchase a tract of farm land and a modern home in the Ozark country. This made a reality of our shared dream to withdraw from the rat race and insulate ourselves against another seizure and incarceration in an asylum.

One day a woman friend and I drove to his secluded location tucked away deep in the Ozark Mountains. I was ecstatic and heartily agreed to wind up my affairs in Chicago. Bill was to pick me up at a future date. He had found employment at his trade in a nearby city and was able to manage the maintenance of this location as a home as well as an investment. Noting his abilities and especially his pleasing personality, one could hardly label him as a candidate for the state hospital. There can be no question that he was a tragic example of injustice.

Unfortunately, when Bill picked me up, he was accompanied by a rather attractive young woman. It was plain to see they were serious about each other, which posed great doubts about our past plans. Ruminating on this while we drove to Detroit on business, I concluded that my exit would be prudent. I disliked the breakup of our relationship. Like a surgeon making an incision, I decided to manufacture an argument designed to make myself disagreeable and hasten the break between us. This act served to alienate the three of us, and in the strained atmosphere Bill sullenly and silently dropped me off in Chicago. He was perhaps confounded by my sudden attitude.

Bill always will remain a true friend to me. I often wondered whether he understood my motive as being a friendly overture in the disguise of a rupture of our association, one that was about as close and intimate as any could be. He was my friend and my decision was based on my desire to see those two happy in a future life unencumbered by my presence. I do miss him and have often regretted our separation. Yet I realize that what I did was meant for his welfare.

A temporary change of jobs required leaving the city for Detroit, Michigan, selling a new product altogether alien to what I had been doing. Since I was given expenses and a modern automobile, I embarked upon this venture, mainly perhaps because of its diversionary nature. As it transpired, I was put under the supervision of a rather domineering and inept sales manager who seemed to think that all sales talent was embodied within himself. For instance, in one case I had a sale in my pocket, but he constantly interrupted my closing efforts. I was furious upon leaving the home and told him in no uncertain terms that I did not in the least appreciate his assistance. Since I had been a sales manager some years before, I was aware of certain basic rules that were never violated. We almost came to blows and I washed my hands of the job.

Driving back to Chicago, I stopped to visit my mother-in-law, for whom I had a certain affection and respect. Her cabin in a town just outside of Chicago was on the route back home. I found her an invalid and quite happy to see me. We engaged in conversation covering the usual amenities. In its course, she suddenly confided in me her wish to reveal information about her own daughter involving our marital life. To my utter amazement, she gave me the true explanation for my institutionalization—my wife wanted me out of the way for the sake of another man. My first reaction was a deep fury, and I am sure that if my wife had been anywhere near me at that time this story would never have been written.

Unfolding before me were recollections of the months of travail and suffering in the insane asylum and her hypocrisy in assuming an attitude of solicitude that was only a ploy to get rid of me and have her unmolested fling. My presence would have meant instant death to the man involved.

The thirty remaining miles to Chicago gave me time to settle my mind and weight the consequences of my actions. I finally concluded that any violent act on my part would have its effect on the children. This consideration alone saved my wife's life, for I fully intended not only to eliminate her but to ring from her the identity of the man and wipe him out as well.

Arriving at my old hotel and seeing good old George served to quiet the tumult that swirled within me. Taking a shower relaxed me to a degree. I phoned my wife, reported my return, and said that I expected her to visit me. I awaited her with a calm fury. I decided to inform her of my knowledge of her perfidy and I derived a certain grim satisfaction from the thought that I could throw the truth at her and tell her to get out of my life forever. Since her own mother's word was irrefutable, all my doubts were dissipated, which created a certain feeling of relief within me. Now love of past days was but a hollow memory and I knew that I must at all cost divest myself of this monster that posed as my wife.

She arrived and I bade her to sit in a lounge chair facing me while I apparently relaxed in bed, setting aside the book I was reading. I began by reminding her of our agreement, prior to our marriage, to settle any possible future differences by the exclusion of third persons that might compromise our relationship. Calmly, I reminded her that she could have had anything she wanted regarding a change in marital status simply by telling me. Finally, I told her frankly that her life was spared only because of the children and that I felt little remorse at the thought of strangling her. To me she was but a reptile that represented all the reprehensible things repugnant to my ideals.

She replied that she loved me, without adding her other amours as well. Bitterly I thought of this love; who in hell wants it, and furthermore, how contaminated must it be. I had the feeling that the garbage man would look askance at it. Finally, I arose and dressed. I accompanied her silently to the streetcar and gladly assisted her aboard, which left me with a sense of relief never before experienced. The truth had shaken me, but its effects lifted the veil and revealed things exactly as they were, without any frustrating doubts, which in the past had gnawed at my very vitals and no doubt contributed to my physical condition.

Returning to my sales work, but with a new firm, my routine was punctuated with interims of forced rest. I moved from the hotel I had grown so attached to, with its many pleasant associations and experiences, and found a modest apartment close to my work. I adopted a strict routine designed to use every available moment to increase my productivity. In addition, I added a kindred line that provided a substantial profit for my endeavors.

The Christmas holidays were approaching and I was invited to my brother's home. My brother, whom I admired for enduring the privations and abuse of our early childhood and which I chose to escape, retained a feeling of obligation to see to it that I had enough to eat, a throwback to our early days, perhaps. But little did he realize that he was endangering my very life by forcing food upon me. Returning to my apartment after the holidays, I began to suffer the same degree of pain as in the perforation of some years before, and I wasted no time going to the hospital. Since the decision to operate was made previously, I was put under the knife again and had a good portion of my stomach removed.

My boss came to see me often, and also one of my colleagues, a lady friend with whom I had been more than intimate for some time. She was quite devoted but, like most women, became possessive and understandably wished to establish a firmer hold to ensure a secure future. Of course, since I was still married, this could not have taken place. Kitty, my amour's name, constantly pursued an aggressive campaign to bring this about. Even if divorced I wished not to enter matrimony feeling that my peculiar background was not exactly suited to its responsibilities. I felt that my future course should be a solitary one.

My wife came to see me at the hospital and found me with a variety of tubes and needles inserted in a number of places in my body. In offering me her gift of flowers and other things, a swell of anger suddenly came over me. Ordinarily, I would have been thankful, but instead it brought to mind the reason for my present condition, and I turned from her in deep aversion. If she had not been so persistent in our original courtship, I felt, when I wished to terminate it, all this would have never taken place.

The time arrived for my discharge and my son came to take me on a trip to Miami, a warmer climate. I thought it nice and considerate and did enjoy the balmy and caressing breezes of the ocean. My son left me to my own desires and I then began the task of finding the job that I must have to maintain myself. To my surprise, the opportunities were extremely limited, and I applied to an appliance firm, having had good prior experience.

On the morning of the first day of work, I had some time to waste, having arisen early for a good start, and I was strolling in the park, dressed neatly, and in no way exhibiting any signs of vagrancy. To my astonishment I was suddenly confronted by two policemen who pinioned my arms and transported me to the lockup. My protests fell on deaf ears, and after a day or two was taken for trial, charged with vagrancy. I was fined a sum beyond my means to pay and, of course, in forfeit taken to the county jail to work it out.

While there, I received among a vast number of letters a notice of my wife's suit for divorce, which gave me a sense of pleasure, for I wanted this to happen. Since she previously had me committed to the state hospital, I suspected she was instrumental in arranging my arrest as a form of reprisal.

I wrote to Kitty for the necessary funds to pay my fine and meantime was incorporated into the jail workforce. This incarceration was not too bad, except for my resentment toward the injustice of it all. I paid my fine with the money Kitty sent and was escorted to the bus station. Two burly deputies did not unhandcuff me until the bus was ready to leave. It was my impression that they regarded me as a public enemy, that I threatened their community with my very being.

11 Settling Down in Southern California

After a prolonged period in bed that brought no relief, I was prevailed on by a friend to go to the hospital for treatment. Having lapsed in my hospitalization policy due to lack of funds, I had no alternative but to throw myself at the mercy of the country, little dreaming that this step would lead to my miraculous recovery.

I spent about seven years with these people, finding them quite congenial. They appreciated my productivity and often gave me bonuses for exceptional achievement. Kitty found it expedient to join me. I was divorced and she mounted a vigorous marriage effort. As the years went by, our intimacy was well established.

My stomach condition had not improved with the operation, and I bore many attacks and enforced periods of rest with adverse effects on my earnings. How could Kitty expect me to marry her in my condition? She dismissed my question with assurances that she would support me. This is the last thing I wanted, and she did not realize how sensitive I was about any woman supporting me. After a violent verbal exchange, I simply asked for a termination of our relationship.

After a prolonged period in bed that brought no relief, I was prevailed on by a friend to go to the hospital for treatment. Having lapsed in my hospitalization policy due to lack of funds, I had no alternative but to throw myself at the mercy of the country, little dreaming that this step would lead to my miraculous recovery.

Arriving at the hospital for admission, I had already assumed that my days were numbered. In truth I was resigned to meet the end, and almost welcomed it as I was weary of the many bouts that wracked me with pain. I was placed in one of the beds on a ward that resembled more a barn, yet its sterile environment lacked even the warmth of a stable.

The resident intern examined me and then informed me point-blank that he was going to cure me. After twenty-seven years of being bandied back and forth by various medicos, I was astonished by this statement. He explained that the cause of my condition was a chronic oversupply of hydrochloric acid and that by removing the connection of the vegas nerve that sent the message to produce the acid, my condition would improve. Skeptical, but with the knowledge that I had nothing to lose, I assented to his operation.

From the start of my convalescence, I began feeling quite free of the gnawing pains of the past, and after a few weeks I was discharged. I felt a surge of well-being within me, and I thought of how I could demonstrate my appreciation for this miracle. Having little money, I selected the finest bottle of Scotch, knowing the propensities of most doctors for stimulation of this type. I expressed my good fortune to have been placed in his care and handed him the whiskey, a pitiful compensation for the service rendered me. He thanked me profusely, adding that this was the first and only gift he ever received from his indigent patients. To this day I regret having lost contact with this young man. I have never suffered a relapse and am able to eat almost anything.

George's wife passed away, leaving him sad and lonely. Coming to see him one day, I found him in tears. In the course of sympathizing with him, he volunteered to pay our expenses to California. Since I had no immediate ties and being captivated by the idea of a more amenable climate, I readily agreed.

In a matter of a few hours the plane brought us to what hopefully would be a new way of life. George had made a reservation at a hotel near the center of the city, where we were at once ensconced and where we assumed a fresh outlook and partook of the daily sunshine and altogether pleasant weather. George, along in years, did not live very long to enjoy the change. He had no childen and in our association over the years I detected a paternal interest in me. I regretted his passing keenly.

The fifteen years that elapsed since George passed away and left me alone are not particularly studded with exciting moments. Mainly, I have found myself continuing to seek that which has eluded me during my past. Alone, with the various members of my immediate family scattered throughout the land, I have felt my isolation requisite in view of the mediocre performance of my life. I believe that my influence might be more retarding than beneficial, so I have chosen the background to avoid embarrassing repercussions.

I have found outlets to ease my frustrations over the years with many hours spent in the poker parlors of Gardena, California, a licencsed city. Together with many sessions of bridge and pinochle, I look back upon them as a pleasant interlude, considering their benefits quite therapeutic. Yet I concede that there are other more sensible and creative activities, some of which I have learned to appreciate. I manage to crash a book from time to time, usually when it is expedient to allow Lady Luck to take a more favorable attitude toward me.

I find time to attend dances and become acquainted with my share of feminine companions, a few of whom almost ensnared me into matrimony. In two instances I escaped providentially. In the first, I discovered the presence of a terrible temper that I could never tolerate, and I wasted no time in making my exit. The second demonstrated a degree of selfishness on one occasion when I was temporarily embarrassed financially, due to an unfavorable turn of luck in a pinochle session. Unable to borrow the necessary sum in time, I presented myself powerless to pay the expenses of our date.

Since a gall bladder operation weakened my heart in the early 1960s, I became eligible for disability and this, together with Social Security payments, has furnished me with the necessities. I've supplemented these earnings with windfalls from my proclivity at games of chance, calculating that I have probably gained far more than I have lost, thus enriching me momentarily in a small way.

Attending the various clubs of Gardena with its drawpoker games, I naturally made more than one pleasant acquaintance, and this blended satisfactorily with my daily routine. Still, this regimen left a void that I found acute, for within me persisted a desire to belong to someone on a more intimate basis. I preferred a woman who could provide me not only with sexual gratification, but even more so with the aesthetic needs that contribute to the justification of living. My affairs from a promiscuous standpoint were few and left me desolate. Their very nature lacked the permanent character of intimacy for which I yearned. Thus, my resort to the gaming tables was more escape than fun.

Growing bored with the way of life I have described, and aware of my needs for intimacy, I became receptive to a woman in the building in which I lived who was widowed a short time before. Attractive in manner and appearance, she piqued my curiosity, and our eventual meeting culminated in a courtship and proposal of marriage. She happened to convey a maternal solicitousness I found extremely agreeable. We both received retirement income, although she also had a nest egg put aside (which did not enter into consideration as far as I was concerned in terms of the proposed union). In short, I wanted a home and mate and was willing to assume the required responsibilities socially and personally.

Unfortunately, this marriage lasted but eighteen months and resulted in a separation, now pending divorce. The break itself was not over a particularly serious matter but largely consisted of an incompatibility that became intolerable, resulting in an inevitable explosion that ended our wedded life.

We are friends and there is no great bitterness involved. She often expresses her disbelief that our happy interim of our marriage has been terminated so abruptly. In view of this, I have been tempted to become reconciled, yet upon sober reflection it is clear that our respective past lives create barriers. Therefore, I accept the choice of isolation, if only to ensure peace of mind from the chaffing of our conflicting personalities.

She faithfully devoted herself to my interests and needs, and I tried to cooperate by accepting the duties of the household with good grace. Compatibility, therefore, becomes a precious factor, all the more rare for those of us who are elderly. Flexibility that promotes adjustment to everyday situations is lost as the years go by. As our bodies stiffen from the erosion of time so, too, our personalities and patience suffers as a result.

The host of many acquaintances, most more casual than intimate, give me a certain richness that serves to spice my daily routine. Today I am altogether free of frustrations and the past doubts and fears have disappeared, so much so that I often amaze myself in assessing my good fortune and enjoyment of my remaining days. Indeed, life is definitely worth the candle, and when I recall the many moments of the past when I doubted the value of existence, I at once feel blessed with my present tranquility.

My present desire is to continue to be active. Still, I am faced with the risk of taxing my energies since I am an intense person in regard to everything. It becomes a matter of prudence to accept retirement. Meanwhile, I find participation in the social routine I follow as being quite fulfilling. I consider my family as being pleasantly devoid of behavior problems, and I live from day to day serenely with the past a rather dim memory. My comparatively good health, considering my age, I count as a blessing.

The crystalization of my present attitudes regarding my past life has brought me to the conclusion that there is nothing I can do except submerge all the unpleasant feelings and regard myself as a casualty of social conditions. The more agreeable aspects of the present crowd out these old memories, and I realize that perhaps many have endured a measure of suffering greater than my own. Also, I understand that a great deal of blame for my suffering can be attributed to failures on my part, exclusive of other influences. I feel today that the mellowness of assuming an attitude of passivity was lacking in the past, and its compensations are constantly brought to my attention.

Although I have complained of various incidents of inequity and injustice in my story, I am quite aware that my past inability to adjust must be taken into consideration. A collective analysis of the many efforts on the part of others to assist me were of no mean proportions, leaving me with regret at my failure to evaluate these benefits and utilize them to create a better result than I have achieved.

It must be confessed that much of my past frenetic turbulance has been neutralized to a great degree. That I am content is beyond question. I recall a curious parallel between my present situation and that of Balzac. Having read his biography, I was impressed by the mental cruelties his mother inflicted on him. That his first intimate relationship was with a woman old enough to be his mother and continued to the time of his death, in spite of his many other amorous experiences, reveals his constant desire for the maternal devotion so lacking in his childhood. I do not mean to imply that I could possibly compare my pitiful literary talent to that great man; I mean merely to concur with his hunger for motherly care that we both lacked.

I still enjoy reading very much and use spare hours to mostly peruse books of a factual nature, although I am not averse to good fiction. Anything of a pornographic nature—the sordid side dealing with perversity in others—does not in the least interest me. This does not mean that I do not relish authentic description of sexual pleasure in good books that come my way.

To conclude this brief statement about my present situation, I would like to emphasize my feelings of peace and tranquility. I presume that most people arriving at age seventy discover this state of mind. The wounds of the past have healed appreciably and all animosity has been replaced by a philosophy of understanding; we all have our burdens to carry and are obliged to appreciate our blessings. At last I have learned the value of friends, family, and good books. Living definitely can be a most enjoyable experience.

12 In Retrospect

I have reviewed the past seventy years of my life, describing the various milestones that represent points of interest along the way. Allow me to remind the reader that my main desire has been to fulfill my obligations and respect to the memory of Clifford R. Shaw and to thank all the other persons that touched me at the crossroads. Who can say precisely what experience fanned the flame within me that burned away the dark shadows and brought about the beautiful vista that is mine today? Really, in analysis, my redemption becomes a collective thing. I remember these things of beauty, savoring in their essence, and drown out the ugly ones. The contrast, I assume, has been necessary to enable me to evaluate the difference.

Perhaps the origin of the inspiration to write my story should be related now. I first met Shaw at age twelve, just after my father died, through the kindly offices of Mr. Cone, my old probation officer from St. Charles. At that time, Shaw was a settlement worker and resided on the premises. The hypocrisy and duplicity so often displayed by some engaged in social work found no place in this man. He fairly exuded sincerity and a cordial warmth that captured my confidence. His entire bearing reflected a certain nobleness that placed him in a category unique among men, and through the years his personality created an indelible influence on my life.

A bit of tribute to the memory of Mr. Cone seems apropos. This courtly gentleman was not motivated just by regulations regarding his duties; rather, he seemed to take more than an ordinary interest in me. To him, I feel deeply indebted, for without the introduction to Shaw, I am confident I would have been another prison number, going through the familiar pattern of incarceration and release. Jane Addams earned her niche in her great work for humanity, but I am sure that Shaw deserves a place at her side for the services he extended during his lifetime in devotion to the human cause.

I began to write my book when I first met Shaw. Subsequently, there were intermittent efforts, and each installment carefully given to Shaw, who in turn supervised the editing to facilitate the narration of my experiences. There was no offer of remuneration and my attitude at that time was a desire to cooperate with him, feeling a sense of obligation to the man who contributed so much to my reclamation. Thus, if some small measure of reciprocity on my part could be exchanged for his help, I eagerly complied.

I am now seventy years old and I owe my good health to the genetic background of my ancestors of European peasant stock. My father died when I was twelve years old, and even though I was away from home for almost half those years, I still revere his memory. He worked hard, often twelve hours a day, as a stoker for the gas company, under conditions that contributed to his death at age firty-one. His early demise fills me with sorrow as I realize that the effects of the long hours of work in the gas-filled chambers hastened his death.

My oldest half-sister once gave me an account of the arrival of immigrants to Chicago. They were transported into the community in great open hayracks to begin their lives with their own kind. Herein they found some security, resumed their native language, attended the same church, and left their offspring the privilege of assuming the American way of life. All the while they suffered the struggle to exist on minimal wages.

In 1912 when I was five years old, I experienced the first of my father's trips to Fred Potthast's saloon on Van Buren Street in the Loop. I sat on a stool and enjoyed the choice of an endless array of meat and cheeses and other viands. My father paid five cents for the lot, including his glass of beer. Truly a wonder bar! The dollar indeed went a long way in those days, but its gain, on the other hand, involved much hardship.

Labor unions were in their embryonic stages at that time. The ten-hour day was very much in vogue, with the average of two dollars per diem the lot of the struggling laborer. In truth he had no choice; either he accepted what was offered or his family hungered.

My father made a contribution to the cause of labor, however, in association with Big Tim Murphy, an early labor boss, by organizing the foreign element in the gas workers' union, one of the first of the period. His union work took place, of course, long before Big Tim acquired the title of gangster, perhaps erroneously so in the strict sense of the word. The truth was that he and my father were fellow workers in the gas company in those early days, and the media classed any labor organizer as an enemy of the establishment.

I am exceedingly appreciative of my father's desire to immigrate to this great country, America. While he bore the brunt of the conditions that affected so many of his contemporaries, I most certainly do not hold him at fault for my childhood delinquencies. Though not the demonstrative type, nevertheless, he tolerated me in his own way.

In my first story and also in this sequel, I constantly refer to my stepmother, placing a great deal of emphasis on the cruel treatment she imposed on my father's children. I do not excuse this, yet, today, I am able to understand its cause. She married my father, in all probability because of the mutual need for a home for her three young children, the exact number represented by my brother and sister and I. The number of older children in the family on both sides were represented equally as a result of previous marriages. Altogether there were nineteen children in the union of these two families.

In reference to the young members and the conflicts that inevitably occurred, a natural preference was given to her offspring, often at undue expense and suffering on our part. I do not condone this past treatment, but I must concede that she assumed a task that required courage and fortitude. I realize that in assuming this burden of responsibility a plus should be added to her account. I do not mean to imply that I now, or ever, held any affection for her. I cannot recall her extending any to us. My brother, my sister, and I, on separate occasions, all ran away from home. That they escaped entirely when able to fend for themselves is a matter of record. We three eventually found a haven in the home of a half-sister, an offspring of my mother's first marriage.

I was never addicted to drugs, and with the exception of a period during a separation from my wife, I have been quite moderate in the use of alcohol and restricted consumption to products of quality. I do my occasional drinking in the home and only sparingly, except when dining out. I consider myself fortunate in this respect, for I have observed the plight of the chronic alcoholic.

As the years went by, I became a habitué of gambling joints scattered throughout the city. Particularly during the depression years, I found this a handy escape and it had deleterious repercussions on my married life. One addicted to gambling is prone to losing not only money but time, energy, health, and possibly one's family. My fascination with gambling was compelling, and I became more proficient with a deck of cards and learned to minimize my losses.

Eventually, I entered the inside sphere and found employment as a croupier. The earnings were lucrative because this profession was not within legal bounds. Gambling houses and horserace bookie joints were numerous and allowed to operate through political protection. Each joint had a direct wire connection that provided patrons with a running account of races at the several major tracks throughout the country.

Observing the law of percentages as a dealer, I learned to be less addicted and more skilled. I was never a *high roller*, to use the vernacular for a big-time gambler. Playing the horses also intrigued me and I suffered the futility of trying to gain from it. After making a study of the hazards, I may today attend a race, but only a few times a year and with no illusions about winning. I have never quite been able to resist the temptation, however, of an occasional game of cards, though I am not as compulsive as in earlier years.

In ending this account, I wish to express my belief that the plight of the transgressor should be alleviated after one has paid the penalty of incarceration. A clean slate and good opportunities to assume a normal life would go a long way toward the solution of many of our social ills. There is no question that the practice of branding these unfortunates should be abandoned for the ultimate benefit of the entire society.

The past seventy years have covered the era of the bustle skirts, the horse-drawn wagon, the old trolley cars with the incessant clanging of the motorman's bell, the wonder of the Victrola and player piano replaced by the miracle of the radio and finally television. Who can deny the great progress made with the convenience of the automobile, and the tremendous strides made in aeronautics? Why then in the face of all this progress should we continue to have problems with people in adjusting to all these wonders? Perhaps the decline in morality can be attributed to our application of these manifold devices.

We must realize that our very existence depends on the continued orderly processes of the cosmos and its relationship to the stability of our earth, an infinitesmial fragment of something so vast that it defies the imagination. I stand humble before all this and believe firmly that there is something beyond our perimeter that promises continued life and that death physically does not necessarily end in tragedy. I know the spirit within me lives and, like the atom, it is indestructible, and I shall continue to live this faith to the end.

Part III
Interviews

13 On Jack-Rolling

Jon Have you done any jack-rolling since the 1920s?

Stanley No, of course! I wouldn't think of doing it today! I would do it first class, go for the big money, use the con game—what do I need force for? I can use persuasion if I want to steal money—I can misrepresent just as well as sell things legitimately.

J. I know this is an unpleasant question, but I want to ask you this: tell me how it feels to you now to have used violence against people in the past.

S. Well, I don't like it.

J. Just go ahead and tell me.

S. Well, I—feel—how would you say it—I feel guilty about it. What else can you say? I don't like to use force on anybody unless it's forced on me. As a matter of fact, I'm just as quick to help somebody that's in trouble physically, somebody that's attacked.

Just like I was at a club, you know, and I was sitting in the game and one of the players jumped somebody else. So I went and grabbed him because he did it without provocation.

So the security guard came over to me and says, "Listen, I don't want you to do that again."

I says, "Why, I was trying to help."

He says, "Don't help us, you're only complicating it! We'll handle these things!"

Well, they have their reasons. I'm just as quick to come to anybody's assistance like that as not, you know. It's repulsive to me to think of hurting anybody. I'm not out looking for trouble.

At the time I was *jack-rolling* I was just a kid and that's the way everybody did it, and I emulated. Now if I were to do it today, I'd be up where the money is. I wouldn't take a chance unless it was worth it, you know. I'm able to evaluate that.

My background was such that there were lots of things that happened during my childhood that led to the development of these instincts. You know, there's a certain air of bravado about a young fellow—where he thinks he's accomplishing something and it doesn't make any difference what it is—even if it's violent—if he's expressing himself as a man. There's part immatureness, part ignorance; immatureness and ignorance are the same thing, I guess.

J.   Do you think jack-rolling is going on today as much as it was?

S.   Well, it's not going on as much. It's going on. Today you have more of the participation of women, B-girls, who are in bars to take advantage of any chance situation that might arise. These women collaborate with the bartenders and give him knockout drops or feed him liquor, and put him in a position where they can take him, see. Then, of course, sometimes they don't have to resort to that—just a woman's natural charm and affection is enough to get the man's attention and to manipulate him for his money.

J.   What about jack-rolling itself—that's still going on, too?

S.   Well, it'll always go on. Why shouldn't it? Aw, of course I don't think it's as prevalent today as it was years ago.

J.   Would it still be called jack-rolling?

S.   Well, they call it mugging. It's the same thing. A mugger is nothing but a jack-roller, that's all, same thing. You have a lot of that in New York. You read about it all the time.

J.   What kind of people were victimized?

S.   Well, of course, those that became intoxicated lay themslves open to being taken. A lot of—especially during prohibition days—there was far more intoxication than there is today. Today, you see, if you come into a bar and show the least sign of having too much, you don't get a drink. But it wasn't that way in those days. They'd serve you if you were lying on the floor. So that was the difference.
    This is without exaggeration: it was a common sight daily, not just isolated days, any given day of the week, you could go down Madison Street and all you would see would be drunks—laying in alleys, laying in sidewalks and hallways—just saturated. As soon as it was legalized in the thirties, there was a measure of control and a change that took place.
    Now you must understand that during prohibition you had a lot of different kinds of bootleg whiskey—not just whiskey but concoctions of all kinds. They sold denatured alcohol, for example, for fifteen cents a shot. They called it *derail*—you could smell it a block or two away, it was so

strong. And there were many toxic cases. They'd drink the stuff out of can; they called it *canned heat*. There was a certain amount of alcohol in there and they would drain it out through the application of fire.

J.   Were there any elderly people around Madison Street when you were?

S.   Oh, an awful lot of them—retired people. You must understand that Madison Street was a haven for people who were maladjusted to a certain extent. A certain number of people found it a haven to hide themselves from the routine that they'd rejected. And then again, some of them were professional vagrants—itinerant workers—who found the economic way of life there more attractive. Although you did have some hotels, even though they were flophouses, all had the sanitation facilities. When you consider that back in the depression you could go in there and get a room for thirty-five cents, take a hot shower, have soap and a towel and everything else, that was pretty cheap.

J.   Were any elderly people ever your victims?

S.   Oh, sure—it didn't matter to me how old they were. I was too young, too immature. Of course, later I got over that, you know, and I've regretted all that. But I was vicious, no question about it, I was just as vicious as any of them.

I don't know what changed me. I almost died in the House of Correction in 1924-1925, and of course, meeting Shaw after that had a whole lot to do with it. I also had a desire, for some reason or other, I can't quite recollect—but it seemed to me that I underwent a change while I was there—not that I was afraid of the consequences of doing time—it's just that I was beginning to awaken to the relative value of things, you see. Of course, I read books, too, and in reading I was able to visualize how other people lived; there were other ways of living than the one I had lived. So perhaps that is the answer, I don't know.

J.   Well, do you think at all about the fact that today you're older and you could be a victim?

S.   Well, I have been a victim already! I got mugged by four or five young fellows; I left a club up on Clark Street one morning about 3 o'clock—this was about twenty-five years ago—and I was walking home. I could see this group of young fellows coming, and I had a premonition; I said, "What the hell, I haven't got anything anyway," although I had a nice billfold, I had $5 or $6 in my pocket, a fountain pen and stuff like that which I treasured and wanted to keep.

J. This was when you were working and were dressed better?

S. Oh, yeah—I was selling, and as a matter of fact a girlfriend gave me this beautiful, lovely billfold as a gift and I treasured it. So as I went past, they corralled me—put the arm on me. I says, "Take it, boys," (laughs)—I says, "whatever I got is yours." They slapped me around a little bit, didn't hurt me too much. I walked away laughing—well, that's the law of compensation—I'm getting a dose of my own medicine. I didn't think anything of it.

J. Do you think about it happening now that you're older and more vulnerable on the street?

S. Well, it just happens that I'm more aware. You see, people don't bother me because I look more capable than the average older person. They're aware that I'm not helpless—not that I couldn't be taken. They also know instinctively that if they do take me they're going to have a fight on their hands.

J. You didn't fight these other guys?

S. (Angry) Where am I gonna fight five people—you misunderstand. When I went past them, they guzzled me. I was helpless. How could I ever overcome five people?

J. But if it's one you'll fight back?

S. One—they'd have a time on their hands.

J. Or two?

S. Two would have a fight on their hands, too. If I hit one and knocked him out, I'd take care of the other one. In the process I'd kick their head in on top of it.

J. What percentage of the men being jack-rolled were homosexuals?

S. Oh, I couldn't quite say—there's quite a few of them on Skid Row, you know, they congregate there just like they do here in Hollywood. They come to Skid Row for the element of impoverished people because most homosexuals have money. Strange as it might seem, homosexuals are usually very intelligent and people of substance. They're productive. Why, I don't know, but that's a known fact. But to have one of them go down on me—I don't like it at all. As a matter of fact, I don't even like a woman to go down on me. It's something against my nature, let's put it that way.

J. The homosexual men—were they always men who were fairly well dressed and better off than the Skid Row types?

S. Usually.

J. Is that right? I had the impression that . . .

S. You have a percentage that are bums, too. It's not confined to the affluent, but the greater percentage of them have something.

J. Were you after both types?

S. You see, you can identify homosexuals by their appearance, because of their apparent affluence in comparison to the general Skid Row population. You wonder what the hell are they doing here on this street? What are they wandering around for, what are they looking for?
   A lot of them are pretty wary. They don't carry large sums of money, so when you get them you don't get very much. They've been taken so much, you know. As a matter of fact, some of the characters they come in contact with are so brutal they put them in hospitals and beat them unmercifully. They not only take their money, but also abuse them physically. I don't think it's right, they can't help it, they're just built that way, that's all.

J. Well, then, were there affluent people who were not homosexuals who were also jack-rolled?

S. Well, if you had anyone of affluence on Skid Row they usually were in business, and they knew the situation, and took care of themselves. Oh, occasionally you might find somebody that would wander into Skid Row out of curiosity—wander into a bar and lay themselves open to being taken—but these were isolated incidents. The common one would be someone that lived in the area, or that worked at some transient job, like a railroad camp, who came into several hundred dollars' pay and got drunk, and laid himself open to being taken for his money. Occasionally you'd find somebody from a normal environment that probably had trouble at home with his wife, or something like that, and came there to try to forget his troubles.

J. Were there ever any women that you jack-rolled?

S. No.

J.   They were all men? Did women get jack-rolled ever?

S.   Oh, they get taken all the time.

J.   But you never chose women?

S.   No, I never did. I never took advantage of a woman in that respect. I wouldn't hesitate to take advantage of them, but not violently, you follow? If I saw a way of taking advantage, chances are I would have in those days. Why not?

14 Los Angeles

Jon So what year was it that you came to L.A.?

Stanley I came here from Chicago with George in 1961. We moved right into the William Penn Hotel when we first arrived. George stayed here awhile and then moved to Phoenix. He bought a home there and died there. He was about eighty-seven or eighty-eight—quite an old man. He was old enough, easily to be my father. As a matter of fact, he was just like a father to me. Lots of times I couldn't pay my rent and he carried me, but I always managed to make it up. If I needed a little money I could get it from him, too. The greatest thing was his interest in my welfare. He never dictated to me. I led my free life and he never questioned me. It was one of these easy relationships. There was nevertheless a feeling of intimacy that suggested that he felt an attachment to me. And of course, I did to him, too. We had a pretty warm relationship.

J. Well, how long did you live in L.A. together?

S. Oh, a matter of months. I was out working in the field, you know, selling music courses and I'd come home on weekends. I got involved in gambling and went overboard. We had a little schism and he got angry at me because he wanted me to make good. I did real well while I was working. We separated for a time, and then he moved to Phoenix. I went there to visit him, but our friendship cooled off after that. Some other man entered the picture and took care of him. This man's influence overshadowed my presence, and I felt as if I wasn't needed anymore, so I left. After I left, he died. George bought a nice home and had a little money. His wife was very good in the stock market, so he probably left a pretty nice nest egg.

I didn't know that he died until long after. Nevertheless, he played a vital part in my life, I mean, he was just like an ace in the hole. But that argument—I just had a bad luck streak gambling, went to the racetrack, and lost my money. I forget just what happened. George didn't like that. He just didn't want me to make a fool of myself. He wanted me to make good—he would have backed me in anything I wanted to do financially.

At any rate, I felt bad that I wasn't around when he died. I didn't stay with him 'til the end 'cause this fellow was taking care of him. George was getting old and senile by that time, and I couldn't reason with him. I wanted to come back and stay with him because I didn't exactly trust this man. I felt that it was my place to protect him, but he wouldn't listen to me. I wanted to get back into his good graces, but I was blocking the traffic, see. So I got out of there.

15 Second Marriage

Jon   So you came out here in the early sixties. When did you meet Sonia?

Stanley   Well, I met her just shortly before I married her—six months before I married her in 1975. Her husband had died a year before that. One day, inadvertently, we had a conversation, and then later I met her on the porch with her sister, and I made some idle remark. We all three wound up in a drugstore and had a sandwich and coffee together. So that's how it started and eventually we married.

I saw her yesterday—we had a nice visit—and everything is all right. I walked with her to the park with the dog and left her there and went on about my business. She still doesn't understand how it all happened. I say (laughs), "Well, if you'd kept your mouth shut it never would've happened."

She says, "You slapped me."

I just slapped her lightly a little bit because she wouldn't keep quiet. She kept yacking and raising hell.

J.   What was she saying?

S.   Oh, something—what we were discussing and she was bringing up stuff and constantly ranting about it and I was—and don't forget, I lost fifteen pounds working and I was run down and I didn't realize I was so run down. I said, Sonia, I want you to be quiet, now. And she insisted, so I said, look—something's got to give, I says, I can't understand this stuff—and I shook her first and then I slapped her lightly—not hard—I didn't hurt her. After all—I just did it to shock her (punctuated with short laughs).

J.   What was she saying?

S.   (Raising his voice) Talking about our affairs—I don't know— ranting about she was doing so much for me and she was buying me clothes and doing this and that. I told her, "Listen, I never asked you to buy me any clothes, and furthermore, I'm not a pimp." I said, "If I want to be a pimp I'd have had ten, twelve broads working for me. I married you because I wanted a home and peace and quiet. I don't want to put up with all this crap every day—you beefing at me. I go out and do the shopping, I do the work,

I do the cleaning, I do this, and I do that—what the hell do you want from me, anyway? Now if that isn't good enough, well, then let's forget about it.''

So when I slapped her she ran out of the house—(laughs)—it didn't hurt her—it wasn't anything, just slight—I wanted to shock her a little, see. I'd never hurt that woman, you know (laughs). She talked about it yesterday—she said, ''You slapped me (laughs).''

''What do you want to do, make a federal case out of it? Look, it's the only way I could shut you up (laughs). You insisted on talking about things that don't mean anything.'' Sure, I'm at fault, I'm not perfect, what the hell. Of course, she realized she was wrong, she admitted it, she's a sensitive woman.

Before this I never touched her, we never had any arguments. This was just like a bombshell when it happened. When she ran out of the house she didn't come back for a week or two. That's when the separation took place. I thought, hell, if that's the way it's going to be, that's the way it's going to be, and that's how it ended.

We had a nice relationship, and we have one still now. I mean, I went to see her yesterday, we discussed our mutual problems, and I fixed some things in the apartment. I'm still tempted to have her forget about the divorce action. But it's in the process already, and she's a funny woman. If she spends any money on anything—she's gonna get her money's worth. She already gave the lawyer a retaining fee (laughs) and she ain't about to lose that. I guess she's gonna go through with it.

J.   She's not interested in a reconciliation?

S.   No, she hasn't talked about a reconciliation at all. As a matter of fact, the way she talks about it, it's all cut and dried, got to go through with it. But she seems to be satisfied that we can be good friends in spite of it. It's not one of those ordinary situations where we bicker and quarrel constantly. She seemed pleased that I came over to see her and did these little things. And she just mentioned briefly that she was going to live with her sister and get the hell out of that place. Her sister's got money, you know, too.

J.   Well, does she have a different point of view about what happened than you do?

S.   The mistake I made in the marriage was that I went to work, and the crux of the whole thing was that she resented that I was working. She didn't want me to work, she didn't think it was necessary for me to work. She wanted me at home, she felt that we had enough income that we could live, which we could have. Maybe I did make a mistake in going out to work (short laugh). What do I need a job for? But I like to be active and the way I feel today, I still want to work.

So the thing is that the underlying reason for her attitude emanated from her desire for me—she felt isolated when I was away working. She didn't mind if I went to Gardena and stayed a day or two, you know, as long as I'd call her. She didn't care, she was pretty good that way, very liberal with me. She never bitched about things, you know, like a lot of women do. "Well, I'm glad you're home, honey . . . . " and she'd have something to eat for me and it was a wonderful thing.

I think I'm throwing something away by this divorce. I'm content with her—she has a lot of wonderful points about her. On the other hand, I like it this way, too. I like peace and quiet. I don't want anyone bothering me (laughs) I want to go and come as I please. So (laughs) I'm faced with a dilemma. I'd like to go back to her, I like the married life, see, but I also like my freedom (laughs)—but you can't have your cake and eat it, too.

It's funny in a way, everybody would look at her like a damn fool (laughs) if she stopped the divorce action. On the other hand, it would be up to me. I'm not crazy about making that move because I like (laughs) this kind of life, too, see. So I'm in the middle—I like it this way, and I like it this way. We got five months before this divorce action takes place. I told Sonia yesterday there's always a chance—I'm leaving it open.

J.   Sounds like you are getting along better.

S.   She's not a hard person to get along with, but underneath it all I'm sensitive. She was the kind of person who would see an ad in the paper, a suit of clothes at Silverwood or Harris and Frank's. "Oh, honey, I want to get that for you." She'd get me shirts and this and that—and I had all I could do to dissuade her from buying those things. I said, "What the hell am I going to do with all this stuff?" I didn't want her to spend money on me unnecessarily. She wanted to show her affection for me in that way. She didn't have to buy me clothes—I knew how she felt about me. She took care of my needs and she wasn't hard to get along with as a rule. However, the burden of homework was on me. I had to do all the shopping, all the cleaning, most of the cooking. But she never complained when I took off—I was free to do so—so the relationship was all right. There was also the factor that she led me to believe that I was under obligation.

J.   To her? How?

S.   Because she has a little money, see. Now because of the things she did, like buying me clothes, she felt as if I was obligated to her. I didn't solicit those things. Whatever my income was, I always contributed to the home, my share, you know. She had her share. I'd go overboard once in a while and she would give me money, but I would reimburse her.

For instance, one time I made a score—I put $500 under her plate and she said, "What's this?"

I said, "I don't know—that's a tip." I won $600 at the racetrack, I gave her $500 and she put it in the bank. I always held up my end. She'd pay the rent, and I'd keep the home in groceries. What the hell—it'd cost $150, maybe $200 a month for groceries. I used to come home (laughs)—I'd break my back sometimes, with $50, $60, $70 worth of—"Where the hell is that stuff," I used to say, "Where is it going?" No end to it. You know, groceries cost money. We had an amicable arrangement. We weren't meticulous about who spent what. I just simply took care of certain things and she took care of certain things and it was a mutual understanding.

J.   But you felt she wanted you to feel obligated to her?

S.   Right!

J.   Was this one of the reasons you were going back to work? Were you trying to have as much money as she?

S.   No. I went back to work because I wanted to do certain things—I wanted to take a trip—I wanted to see my family. I didn't want to ask her for the money. I'm funny that way. She's got a little money. If I need a few dollars, I'll compensate her in my next check, but that's as far as it goes, see. The only thing I asked her for was the car when I went back to work. She bought the car. I was making enough money that I could easily have paid her for the car within a month or two.

J.   You wanted to take a trip to see your children and grandchildren?

S.   I wanted to see the children—yeah, and I wanted to be active, too, through working. I got tired of Gardena. I wanted to get away from gambling and get active and be productive. I enjoyed it. Unfortunately, it ended the way it did.

J.   Going back to work put a lot of pressure on you?

S.   Well, it put a lot of pressure on me because she resented it because I wasn't home as much. I'd be home ten, eleven o'clock at night, where ordinarily I'd be home earlier, be home at supper. Now, she never knew when I was coming home. I might have calls to make that kept me out there.

She wasn't feeling well, either. Her hearing is going bad. She was having trouble with her back. She's a hypochondriac; she has medicine bottles all over the place. Pills here and pills there and going to the doctors all the time. So I think that her physical condition had a whole lot to do with the breakdown, together with the strain that was being placed on me in working, among other things.

I'd come home and I'd get all this gas, you know, and it would get on my nerves. If I wasn't working I would pass it off, you see. When you're out working, it takes something out of you—you don't have the capacity to absorb that stuff. When you get through selling, you want peace and quiet, because you've had enough of people, right (laughs)? You want to sort of relax and take it easy and give yourself a break.

If you come home and listen to a woman ranting at you all the time, it's too abrasive. But it isn't her fault (laughs). She didn't want me working, and I didn't have to be working. So, she has a point. But I felt this way, if I wanted certain things I thought it was my place to earn them, not to ask her for the money. Just because she has a little money put away doesn't mean that I have to take advantage of her. That's her money, not mine. I didn't marry her for a few dollars, you know.

J. How much money does she have, may I ask?

S. Oh, she's probably got $30 to 40,000—not a hell of a lot.

J. That's not a lot? In savings?

S. Well, she's got most of it in trust.

J. Does she have children by her previous . . .?

S. She doesn't have any children. She has $5,000 put aside for me (laughs). Well, I didn't ask her for it—she probably cancelled that already. I don't care about it. To me, I can live the rest of my life with the income that I now have. If I want any extra money I'll go out and hustle. I can sell and make extra money. But if I do that, I have to forgo my disability. But that doesn't mean anything—the disability payments don't mean anything in comparison to what I can earn when I work. It's just a question of whether I'm physically able to manage.

J. In addition to the money she had in savings, she had Social Security, too, right?

S. Oh yes, she has good Social Security.

J. How much was it?

S. $290.

J. And did she have any other regular income?

S. Well, I told her to get disability, too, because of her age. She got that, so she gets $370 a month.

J. And what was your income?

S. Now before I got married I was getting $164, plus my Social Security—close to $300. What do you think my income here is now? $130 Social Security and $87 disability.

J. It went down?

S. Because of the marriage—but they're making an error at Social Security. I'm entitled to a budget of approximately $300, and I'm only getting $217. I have to pay $135 a month rent here, don't forget and that's not enough money for me.

J. So how are you making up the difference that you need in order to pay your bills?

S. Well, I'm struggling along. It's tough. I don't have enough from Social Security to pay the rent, I have to take $5 from the $87. I have to pay for my food, telephone, clothes, and other expenditures. If it weren't for the fact that I can hustle a little bit in cards to buy some groceries, I'd starve to death.

J. So how much would you say that you make at cards?

S. Oh—there's no way of knowing—I win and I lose, you know. But I win more than I lose. The difference is enough to keep me existing. I don't go into debt, and I don't owe anything.

16 Law Suit for Wages

Stanley I'll describe, for example, this suit that I have against a music company that owes me wages. Now there is something to dwell upon. How can a man who's a millionaire disregard my rightful wages?

Jon Perhaps that's how he got to be a millionaire?

S. Yeah, but he ain't gonna get away with it with me. He ain't gonna have many music schools if he keeps on not wanting to pay me. I'll guarantee you that. I'll turn out to be a criminal, if I have to; to get justice. I won't let him get away with it.

My old man came over here to get away from tyranny and that sonofabitch is not going to perpetuate it because he's a millionaire. It's not because of the money [$300.00], I can get along without it. I've lost that much at the racetrack. It's the idea that I lost fifteen pounds of flesh and blood by working to achieve that money, walking between calls. And he has the nerve to say that he doesn't want to pay me? He ain't gonna exploit me! I'm gonna kill the sonofabitch, if I have to! I mean it, too! I don't go for that!

J. You're going to try to recover legally through the Department of Labor?

S. If I can't get legal recourse, I'm going to shoot him in the head. Oh, no! There's no room for this sort of thing. If I went and stole anything from him, wouldn't he put a gun to my head and kill me?

I think his stand is very unreasonable. I've never had an agreement like this with any music school in all the time, the twenty-five years, I've been doing it. I don't see why he should live off my endeavors. The custom has been over the years that after you have enrolled a student in a course, that you are paid immediately, the full commission. It's a two-way street, I don't get anything out of the instrument sales, right? He might sell an instrument for $500, $600, $700 dollars and make $300, $400, $500 profit. He doesn't say here, Stanley, here's—. So he's got to take the bitter with the sweet, and that's been the common thing with all these schools.

He's brought up these conditions having never told me about them before he hired me—they don't have a phone or this and that. What the hell difference does it make if they have a phone if they come to the school and bring their money? It's potential, right?

You know what he said to me? "I feel sorry for you," he sat there pompously.

"I don't want you to feel sorry for me," I said, "don't worry about me," I said, "just give me my money, that's all I'm interested in." Feels sorry for me (laughs), I don't know what he intimates, as if he thought I was crazy to make this kind of complaint with the labor board. Well, where else am I going to go with it?

Here's another thing, I said, "with this, prepare yourself to go all the way, because I'm going to carry you all the way to the Supreme Court on this." I said, "I've never been . . . People have always paid me for any work that I've done. It's a matter of principle—the amount of money is negligible. He sat there and looked at me. He's got sixteen schools and he's trying to beat me out of. . . .

17 The Taxi-Driver Squabble

Stanley Sonia only lives a few blocks away, you know, four or five blocks. I can go over there and have dinner or stay all night if I want anytime. Except, the landlady, for some damn reason she's got a yen against me. Now, I don't know what I did, besides one time they were trying to get in a cab over there, those old women in the building, you know, and I had called a cab the day before. I never could get 'em, they would say they're coming and they would never show up, you know.

So, this fellow, it was the same outfit, I commented about the service, it was so lousy. I said, "How come you fellows don't come over and get me when I call?" He gave me some snide remark, and I didn't like it. I kinda told him off, you see; I might have used some rough language in the process. That old woman downstairs told my wife she said, "I don't want him in the building anymore" (laughs).

I didn't do anything to her, I was talking to the cab driver. He got me mad. I said, "You say another word I'm going to hit you and push you right over that . . . and I would've too, I was mad at him because he was so snotty about it!

Jon What did he say about why they wouldn't come?

S. Well—I forget—whatever he said it wasn't very complimentary. And he rubbed me the wrong way, you see, and he acted a little pugnacious about it. I said, "If you feel that way about it, maybe you'd like to go over that cab!" I said, "If I ever hit you hard enough that's where you'll go, right over that cab!" (laughs). He's a young fella, kinda husky too but I was so damn mad I wanted to kill him (laughs).

I wanted a cab in the worst way the last time. I don't know if Sonia was going somewhere, but they kept telling me: "The cab will be there, the cab will be there"—and the damn thing never did come. So, I was pumped up about it, see. And he acted as if, "Well, what the hell, it's an every-day—well, what's the difference, who the hell are you that we should get a cab for you?" But I shouldn't have gotten concerned about it, I shouldn't have even said anything about it. That's where this passivity business comes in. One has to learn to prevent that sort of verbal altercation. I'm using that now and it's effective—I don't have near as much trouble as I used to.

J. Can you give me an example of when you've been able to exercise restraint and avoid conflict?

S. Well, I do it constantly. People irritate me, I don't flare up, I stop, and think. I study the situation and how inadvisable it is; get all pumped up for what? It only complicates the situation. It's better just to be quiet and ignore it, you know. I'm learning. At my age (laughs) it's a hell of a . . . but I'm getting there. I'm telling you it's tough sometimes, some people burn me up. It's getting so I don't react as much mentally because I'm prepared, you know. Even though I may seethe inside, I'm developing a natural habit of toleration. Of course, after that person is out of sight, I chew 'em up inside. To myself I say, "That sonofabitch, I should've broke his neck," or something like that—I let it out of me when I'm alone. I refrain from it while the person is there.

J. Is there a noteworthy instance where you didn't react aggressively?

S. Well, nothing, uh (long pause).

J. That's okay.

S. I can't recall any particular, generally, you see, I don't have many incidents like that. In the past when I did have them, I used to get pretty stormy at times, and I didn't hesitate to tell people off about what I thought of them. Now in analyzing myself, I realize that it's not the other person's fault, but my exacting requirements.

J. What do you mean by "exacting requirements?"

S. About their behavior—about their reaction. What I mean is, when people seem to get unreasonable in their attitude, I was prone to resent it very much. I'm getting so that I understand it. Everyone is capable of that sort of thing and I have to learn to roll with it intsead of getting unduly concerned about it. There's nothing you can . . .if I do make an issue out of it, I only get worked up, and it's not good for me, and it doesn't improve the relationship. A little diplomacy I find later I feel pretty good about it—I acted pretty good there—you know it pays off (laughs). At seventy years of age, you know (laughs) I'm getting wisdom (laughs heartily). Hell of a long time isn't it!

18 The Gardena Card Club Encounter

Jon Tell me about this security officer at Gardena who hit you.

Stanley Well, I think it was a case of mistaken identity, see. You know, they go by initials there. They have a board, and they put your initials up in order and call you when there's a seat open for you. When they allude to you, you're J.C. or M.P.M. or whatever it is, you know. It happened that I came there one evening and I'm having coffee in the Monterey Restaurant adjoining the card club. I was talking to the person next to me, and all of a sudden security came in. They said, "You're making a lot of noise!"

I said, "What?" I been going there for years, I've been giving them my money, you know. Don't forget, they tap me on the shoulder every half hour for money. It's just like working for them when I'm gambling.

J. How much do you have to pay?

S. It all depends on the stake. You pay so much according to the limit, see. The higher the limit, the higher the rate.

J. Give me an idea.

S. Well, if you're playing $1 and $2 limit, you're paying $1 every half hour. If you're playing $2 and $4, you're paying $1.25; if you're playing $3 and $6, you're paying $1.75; if you're playing $5 and $10, you're paying $2 a head, and so on. There's many a day that I spent ten, fifteen, twenty hours in the place; the entire time they're open. So suppose I spent twenty hours in the place and I give them on the average $2.50 per hour. That's $50 a day that they collected. How many days have I done that? I've been going there for years, and I never had any serious trouble. I never cheated anybody. I've had my share of small arguments, which you're bound to have in card games where you have contention, but they didn't amount to anything.

I never was enthusiastic about the idea of cheating at cards. To me the fun of cards is in the challenge of winning. If you cheat, you lose the challenge, the essence of the whole thing. Sure you want to make money, but that isn't all there is to it. There's a lot of skill in cards, and if you resort to cheating, well the skill isn't necessary, so it loses its fascination.

So now when the security came in, I said, "What are you talking about, what do you mean 'disturbance'?" In the meantime, another security officer came in and he hovered over me and I said, "What do you want? What are you doing," I said, "ganging up on me? What, did I commit a crime, or what? I'm just here having a cup of coffee." I said, "I'm not bothering anybody!"

All of a sudden, wham, he hit me in the jaw. Of course, that's simple assault and battery and that constitutes liability right then and there. They have no right to do it, whether you are wrong or right, see. I was so mad, I said, "Don't come down tomorrow, I'm going to shoot you right in the head." I was going to get a pistol and kill the sonofabitch. And I meant it, too!

In reconstructing this thing later, I figured that I am too good of a customer for them to bar me the way they did and for striking me for no reason at all. When they barred me, I said, "If you feel that way, I'm going to sue you." At first I wanted to forget about it because the floorman and I were pretty good friends, and he came and straightened it out. He told me to see the floor manager across the street in the Rainbow Club the next day. As I pushed in the door on the following day, the floor manager is there with his hands up, and says, "You can't come in here, J.C., you're barred." I said, "You feel that way about it, well, fuck you! I'm going to sue you!"

Now J.C., I found out later, looks a lot like me and he's a trouble maker, and they want to get him out of there. So they have confused me with J.C., which I have discovered only in the past couple of weeks. I was on the bus talking to a friend of mine and he says, "You look a lot like J.C.; you could be taken for twins." But this doesn't make any difference, they have no authority to come in and strike you. Their recourse is to call the police whether you provoked it or not.

J. Were you hurt at all?

S. Well, it didn't do me any good, it was right after I had this auto accident. I was having dizzy spells then, and this guy weighs one hundred and ninety pounds and he hit me flush on the jaw. Now is that going to help me any, if I'm having dizzy spells already? I'm still having dizzy spells. They come intermittently and last until I rest.

J. What do the doctors say?

S. Well, what do they know, it's an ambiguous thing, it's hard for them to determine.

J. What do your lawyers say about the suit?

S. They say I have a case, allright. They're pursuing it!

19 Friends

Jon You're friends with some of the men in the park?

Stanley You don't call those friends, they're not the right kind of people. I'm getting away from that. You can't be nice to those people—they take advantage of you. I've tried to help one fellow—75 percent of his liver is gone—he's got a boyfriend who's got this station wagon. Now he's been bleeding me for whiskey. The other guy, I've been bringing him food for over a month now. I don't mind helping him because he's got this liver condition, you know. But every time this other guy would see me: "You got enough for a pint," "You got enough for a half pint," "You gonna buy a bottle" of this and that. At first I was easy with him. Finally I said this is it, where am I going to get the money to support your habits? They take advantage of you.

Oh, there are some nice fellows over there, but the really nice people don't cotton up to you, they usually discriminate about who they take up with. Now you can take up with anybody there, but the chances are 95 percent that they're gonna try to exploit you in some way. So the best thing to do with those kind of people is to keep away from them. So I'm glad I am the hell away from that neighborhood.

J. Well, do you have some other friends?

S. Well, I don't know what you'd call a friend—I call them acquaintances. I've had a lot of disappointing experiences trying to make friends, especially those I've gambled with and are hard up on their luck and busted. They turn on you. They take advantage of you. Of course, when I look back on it now I've probably taken advantage of people myself so who am I to complain? Some of them are so bad they think you're a sucker. When I come to the realization that they feel that way, I get mad. I get really hot. They are brutal about the way they take advantage of you.

J. Can you give me an illustration?

S. Well, for example, this fellow that was sleeping out in the park. He was sleeping in a canopy of cable spools by a Korean Church. He's dedicated his life to drinking wine. I felt sorry for him. I got the idea, well, maybe I can help him if I can bring him food and if he'll eat enough maybe he won't drink so much.

His boyfriend is nothing but a thief—well, they're both thieves, both were in the penitentiary, excons. But this little guy that's sick, he's got principle about him. The other guy turned out to be nothing but a hustler. He was hustling me and it took me a month to find out. Everytime he'd see me, have you got money, and with him it was Scotch, you know, it wasn't wine.

I didn't mind buying the other guy a bottle of wine, I knew he had to have it. But now I've got my last ten-dollar bill, this is several weeks ago. I'm sitting' in the station wagon, and he says, "You gonna buy," he was sittin' with his girl.

I says, "What the hell's the difference?" Get Jimmy his wine, that's sixty-eight cents, and it'll be about $2 for a half pint of Scotch for him, so it'll cost around $3 altogether. What do you think he brought me back? The sonofabitch went and bought a pint of Scotch and gave me $3 change, knowing it was my last money.

Now you see how sensitive I am, I don't care about helping buy the whiskey, but when he is so careless as not to consider me, I felt like taking him, as big as he was, and pushing him through the windshield. In other words, I realized I was a sucker. So I fumed. I didn't say anything. I exercised control. I said, "I don't feel too good, take me home."

I got home and for two or three days I seethed inside. I just couldn't take it. I must of spent, I don't know how much money—given money for gas, for food, did a lot of things for both of them. I came around the park the last time, he ignored me, he was afraid to come near me. He knew damn well I was mad. He didn't even say hello to me. He kept away from me and it was a good thing he did because even as big as he was, he was fooling with dynamite.

J.   It sounds like you're saying that this has happened before?

S.   Well, it's happened a few times. The way I look at it today, there is no necessity for me to do that. If people need help, they don't need me. They can go to the relief agencies and get assistance, what the hell do they need me for? Why should I give them of my income, for what? I'm a damn fool, that's all?

J.   Stanley's Mission?

S.   Yea, I'm a mission (laughs). What hurts, it isn't that I miss what I give them, I don't care about it. It's just that I realize that I am being taken. They take advantage of me. Those people are adept at putting you on. They have a way of manufacturing reasons for you to help them more. They make a profession of it, let's put it that way.

Who was it that said, or is it just an old saying, that you go through life and die and if you wind up with one good friend, you're fortunate. I don't think that a real friend is easy to find, we look for friends. Appreciating that I am living alone, I must naturally strike out for some sort of an outlet emotionally, right? I've got to feel that my existence is justified to some extent, I can't just live for myself. But on the whole, at least 90 percent of my efforts to be giving in my small way are futile. I haven't got much to give, but if I am to be altruistic, I usually become disillusioned in the process. I don't understand why. I have that inclination to do things for people and to hunger for, I don't know what, how would you describe it?

J. Companionship? Intimacy?

S. That's right, but at the same time I'm sophisticated enough, you see, I've been through enough of this grifting and grabbing and stealing and begging and all that crap to know the difference. And when I am being taken, I really get hot. When I feel as if they are imposing on me . . .

J. Sounds like it takes you awhile, though, to realize what is going on.

S. Well, you have to give everyone a fair trial. But you see, I am not in a position to give anybody a fair trial, I have all I can do to take care of myself. I've come to that full realization today. I'm getting hard about it. I don't want to help anybody, because I don't want to get hurt, you see. It isn't that I dislike helping, I just don't want to get hot, and one of these days I'm liable to maim somebody and put 'em in the hospital; they get me so mad. There is more callousness in this town than I've seen in any other city. There seems to be some sort of mass psychology among certain elements of the people where they think they've got it coming; that they're entitled to live off of someone else.

J. Is this realization recent?

S. Oh, yeah! Anybody stops me on the street today and asks me for a dime, I'd turn 'em down cold. Unless, I saw 'em laying there suffering, with their tongue sticking out (laughs).

J. Really desperate?

S. They'd have to be really desperate! You see, you can only stand so much. I paint myself as being a sucker!

J. Well, have you had friends, like George, that you especially liked?

S.   Well, of course, Shaw was my real friend. But I can't say I can count too many I would call a friend. Alot of acquaintances but few genuine friends.

J.   Has it been easier for you to be friends with women than with men?

S.   Well, I don't know. Naturally, I'm getting to the age where the sex impulse is not quite as strong as it used to be. I do find that there are few women I can cotton up to as true friends. The average woman, if she is going to be your friend, and there are exceptions to the rule, they have a motive. They want you to marry.

   I prefer the company of men over women. Women are so emotionally constituted that they are not as easy to get along with as are men. I find it much easier to get along with men, although I have my differences with them. I run into disillusionment. I find out their trying to take advantage of me in some way, and I get hot. You know what I do with those kind of people, I just shut them off immediately. I don't have anything to do with them whatsoever.

   I had this one woman before I was married, a nice-looking woman, had a little class to her, and she was liberal as far as being intimate was concerned. I forget what she did now. She was a reformer. She rubbed me the wrong way. Finally, I said to her, "Listen, you and I are not compatible, let's forget about this before it goes any further for our own mutual good."

   I will say this. Perhaps, I resent being controlled by a woman. There may be a deep-seated reason, my background. I feel as if it is not a woman's place to dominate a man.

J.   Have you ever had a friendship with a woman that was not sexual?

S.   Well, I had it once. We were friends. I met her at a dance and made a date with her and went to the race track. We had dinner and went to the hotel. She laid on the bed, and I'm breaking the track record getting my clothes off. She was built for sex, if anyone ever was. First time in my life I couldn't get an erection, and there wasn't a damn thing I could do about it. There wasn't anything she could do about it. It was inexplicable. You know, I'm mystical about those things, so I said, "From now on, you're my sister. I'm not supposed to lay you, because If I do I know I'm going to knock you up sure as hell." There was a reason for this. I don't know what it was. This had never happened to me before. So, I went with her for months at different times, never touched her. She was a good friend. Usually when I went out with a woman, I always wanted to get in her pants. After all, I was separated and that was my objective.

J.   In this one instance, however, the reason you became friends was because you couldn't have a sexual relationship?

S. Well, I could have had sex if I'd wanted to, but I decided not to. It wasn't that I wasn't capable of doing it later, it was just an isolated instance. I just felt it wasn't my place to pursue her in this respect, whatever the reason.

J. So what happened to this friendship?

S. Oh, she got engaged. I said, "Well kid, I'm not going to block the traffic." Besides, I wasn't divorced anyway. I was always on the lookout after the separation to try to find the right woman. I always looked.

J. Did you ever have a friendship with a man that was sexual?

S. Well, not really. Oh, when I was kid on Madison Street there were "fruits." I had relationships with them. I didn't like it, I didn't like it at all. We used to exploit them, you know. It was sickening to me. I couldn't stand it. Of course, in institutions you have your share of masturbation; all kids do that more or less, I guess. But I was retarded sexually. I didn't develop until I was fifteen or sixteen. I had a penis on me about this big (indicates about two inches). It took time for me to come to fruition. After I left the House of Correction, I began to have an appetite for girls. When it comes to men, its unnatural.

20 The Sunset Bar Scene

Stanley   I am not addicted to alcohol to the point where I must have it; it all depends on my mood. Sometimes, for no reason at all, I might walk into a bar because I want to sit there and relax. So I have a drink or so and walk out. And once in a while I'll go overboard and have three or four drinks, and maybe one too many. When I start getting dizzy, I stop myself and get out. I have something to eat usually, and that neutralizes it. I'll get in a cab and go home. But lately (laughs), I usually wind up in some kind of a fracas. Somebody wants to fight me. It isn't that I want to fight them, they want to fight me. I don't know why. I can't figure it out. I don't understand it.

I was in a bar up on Sunset here a month or so ago. I'm feeling all right, I'm drinking good Chivas Regal at $1.50 a pop; I've got money, I drink the best, the hell with it, I believe there's only one time you go around, you might as well go around in style. And I always leave a tip for the bartender, too, you know. To me, that's the way we did it in gambling circles—we have the best and we live the best. That's the way I was brought up with those people and a lot of that has rubbed off on me. Now I don't necessarily have to live that way every day, but I retain that inclination, if you follow what I mean.

So, anyway, I'm in this bar right here in Echo Park, so they change shifts. Now the one that was on was a pleasant one. But the other one's a crabby bastard, and for some reason or other she don't like me. Well, I can't help that, you know, if they don't like me, they don't like me. So that's her prerogative—I don't take issue with that. Maybe there's something about me that's unpleasant, so they're entitled to that view.

She's very nasty about the way she's serving me, for no reason at all, you know. Finally she got too nasty about something and I said, "Listen, I'm spending my money here," and I said, "Am I bothering you, am I stealing anything from you? What are you givin' me that lip for?" I says, "Who the hell do you think you are?" I says, "When you talk to me you talk to me with respect and I don't give a goddamn whether you've got a cunt or a prick on you, see." And I had enough booze in me that I didn't care, you know. I wasn't drunk. I knew what I was doing.

Jon   What had she been doing to you?

S.   I forget what it was, she was just unreasonable, you know, just abusive.

109

J. She wasn't serving you right?

S. She was just . . . tryin' to treat me like a piece of shit, let's put it that way.

J. She was abrupt?

S. No (exasperated)—she had a boyfriend in the corner—now let me finish so you'll get the picture. He was in the corner. She's talkin' to me this way because she's got somebody there to protect her, see. Or that's what she thought, anyway. Finally, she said one word too much and I said, "Listen, you bitch." I says, "You say another goddamn word, I'll throw this goddamn drink right in your face and kick your cunt in on top of it." I says, "You don't talk to me that way. I'm a customer here, I'm not a piece of shit." I says, "I give you $2 a pop for a drink. Does anybody else come in here and pay that kind of money?"

J. What did she say?

S. (Mimicking) uhhhhhhh—and her boyfriend got up and he comes after me, see. Now he weighs about one hundred and ninety pounds, but fortunately when the sonofabitch came at me I happened to get him just right, and he kind of toppled halfway and when he did I gave another one and he went down like the Titanic.
   I weighed one hundred thirty-six pounds that day. I'll never forget, I weighed myself. I kicked his fuckin' head in. I kicked him unmercifully. He was just lucky I didn't have these shoes on, I'da killed him and I didn't give a shit. But I had those light tan shoes on and I just kicked his face in and his head and I wanted to kill the sonofabitch. That's how I felt because all this is unwarranted. I didn't do anything to bring this about, see. That bitch come out there and got to work and taken my money and ringin' it up on the cash register and insultin' me, and I'm a businessman? I'm a salesman and I don't know the difference between etiquette in business and not?
   She's a miserable sonofabitch. She ran out, called the police. I says, "You miserable sonofabitch," I says, "call the morgue," I says, "I'm gonna kill this cocksucker." And I says, "If you don't get out of my way, I'm gonna kill you, too, you dirty bitch." And I found out he was in the hospital. I didn't kill him, but he was in pretty bad shape.
   Now you see, I laid myself open to gettin' killed. I was just lucky that I happened to hit him just right so that he swayed a little bit and then I was able to give him another. I got a pretty good punch, you know, for one hundred thirty-six, especially with my right, see. And when he went down, I didn't waste any time to see that he wouldn't get up to try to finish me

because after all he had the advantage of sixty pounds of weight. So who's kiddin' who about what? So I was afraid after—she was out screamin', "Police."

I walked out and took the roundabout way through the alleys so the cops in the squadcars wouldn't see me. They'd know who I was right away from the description. I went home, I never heard anything about it. One of the boys in Echo Park says the guy is in the hospital. I says, "I hope the sonofabitch dies," I says, "I don't have any fuckin' use for him because he didn't have any respect—he wanted to kill me, that's what he wanted to do."

If they happen to hit me first, then I go down, and I can't get up. So, temporarily I retreat (laughs), but as soon as I get up, I go after them again (laughs). I never give up. They gotta kill me, that's all. I'm just built that way. I was brought up to hate my stepmother for abusing me, and any sonofabitch that abuses me in my life gets the same attitude. I carry that over. Now, if I do something that's wrong, I think I'm fair enough to admit it, and I'll take the punishment for it, without retaliation. But the moment I think I'm being stepped on, that's all, I just don't take it.

J.   This is happening more often now you say?

S.   Well, it did happen quite a bit. It happened a week ago up at the Horsehoe Club. I was playing poker and holding my own, about $17 or $18 ahead, and the guy sitting next to me complained that I was stepping on his foot. I said, "Well, I didn't realize it." I was talking nice to him. It just happened that a couple of hands before I got into a hell of a pot, six-way action, I had two pair, kings and tens, and there were raises. I won this big pot, and this sonofabitch next to me was in the pot. He got nasty, "You been steppin' on my foot all day long," he says, and "I don't like you," he says. He was giving me that hillbilly bullshit. He stood up, he was going to take a poke at me (laughs). I got him. Before you know it, his glasses fell off, and as soon as I hit him, the blood gushes out of him (laughs). I got hold of him by the neck and I was giving him the business in the body. Then the security came and separated us.

Now you see, he started it all, he got up to try to fight me. He wanted to take a poke at me for no reason at all. So, they asked me to leave, and take my checks, but I said, before I leave I want you to find out from the table who's at fault here, who instigated this. So, the players say that this fellow started it all. But I got chased out and that sonofabitch stayed there. So that's justice. He's bleedin' and he caused all the trouble and they chase me out, see. Why is it that I get the dirty end of it?

J.   Did you get barred there?

S. Well, it only lasts for awhile, it blows over, you come back and they forget about it.

J. So why is it happening more often now than before?

S. I don't understand, except, there is something about the character of this city and the people. I'll be honest with you, I'm circumspect in how I deal with people. I try to back off and try to guard against things like this and not get abrasive or abusive and try to give 'em a soft answer to start with. Now, if that doesn't work, and they insist on getting rough, I'm not going to run to the guards. I'm not a stoolpigeon, I'm not built that way, I handle my own affiars. If the guards can't see this coming up before it culminates into something, who's fault is it? It's theirs, isn't it? They can come and stop it before it gets to that point.

I don't want this reputation of being a fighter and a tough guy. I'm not a tough guy at all. I want to get along with people and do the right thing, but I don't want them to step on me unnecessarily either, because if they do, I'm not going to stand for it. Where I fail is in forestalling—I should check myself—and weigh the consequences of my attitude of retaliation. I must learn to be more tolerant, and allow these things to pass over, because nothing is gained by it. I lose by it, in more ways than one. So, I'm trying now to keep away from it as much as possible, but it's gonna be a hard job (laughs). It's a habit that's going to be hard to break (laughs).

J. How are you trying to break it?

S. By being just humble, give in, give them a soft answer. At my age it's necessary that I become flexible. It's not becoming for me, a man seventy years old, fighting like a brawler.

J. Yea, but the feeling humble is also hard for you to take.

S. Well, yes, but it has its compensations. I don't really care what people think. I can be humble to a man and he can say to me, "You're a coward." I'll take it, but don't let him lay a hand on me because if he does (laughs), I won't go for that. The humbleness goes out the window then, and we go into action. However, I'm over seventy, it's time for me to get some sense in my head. What the hell am I gaining by all this brawling, what am I trying to prove, where am I going? So it's got to be that I capitulate, and take a different attitude. I have to learn how to back away, that's all. I'm learning and it's a good feeling, but why should it have taken so long?

And I'd like to know why it has been happening so much. I don't understand it! I don't get into conversations in bars, except with the bartender. I sit and drink and mind my own business, and when I get through, I'll get the hell out of there. I've talked this over with my friends. It's baffled me. I've found out that it's much better not to drink in a public place. So, I must do my drinking at home.

J.   This never happens when you're not drinking?

S.   Well, very seldom. Do you think for a minute that afterwards I liked kicking this guy's head in? I didn't feel good at all about it, I wondered if the poor bastard was dying. I wondered if I'd killed him.

Here's another thing. When I find myself being passive by restraining myself and weighing the consequences, I get such a feeling of satisfaction, it's immeasurable—it's something altogether foreign and different and nice and pleasant and in contrast to the reaction of being violent. After you're violent with somebody, you begin regretting—what the hell did I hit him for—you go through another kind of turmoil.

By being passive, there's a feeling that comes over you that's good. It's better for me to be passive. So, now I'm faced with the choice: Do I want to feel better or do I want to feel worse? If I take the right choice, I'll defeat that which has troubled me all my life. It's working.

J.   But, you're telling me it's happening more often now.

S.   Naw, I haven't had any trouble, it just happened in the card room. I couldn't help that. What would you do if he got up to take a poke at you? I suppose, if I let him take a poke at me and I didn't do anything about it, then security comes and chases him out, right? But I sit there like a damn fool and everybody thinks I'm a coward because I don't protect myself. But, I'm beginning to feel the wonderful effects of being passive. You know the Bible has a saying, "A soft answer turneth away wrath." So when someone annoys you, that soft answer throws them off more than if you'd argue with them. It's taken me a long time to arrive at this.

21

Visit to Chicago

Jon You took a trip to Chicago?

Stanley Yeah. I was amazed at the cleanliness of the town. The streets were clean and I enjoyed walking down Michigan Avenue and noting the shops and the architecture that's been erected since I was there fifteen years ago. See, I was trying to contact certain people and wasn't able to find too many. I tried to get hold of McKay and he's moved out somewhere, and Hetta has moved out of Batavia. I don't know what's happened to her. And I wanted to see Anthony Sorrentino. He's working for the state, but he happened to be out to lunch or out somewhere. He was to come back again but still hadn't come back so I didn't get a chance to talk to him. Time goes by and they have a whole new crowd at the Institute. No one there anymore that I know.

But I did enjoy my grandchildren, two of them, and my boy has a nice home and seems to be well adjusted. He's fortunate in having a good wife that's just the right person, for him just what he needs. He has his problems though. I think it is his biological background, he's just built that way, that's all. It could be attributed also to scarlet fever he had when he was little. He had an awful siege of it.

J. What kind of emotional difficulties does he have?

S. Well, he gets depressed, you know, intermittent periods. Being the oldest, he's not as far advanced as the other two are, as far as economic success is concerned. One boy, he's so talented, he can just about do anything that he wants to. He's been loaned to the Saudi Arabian government as an airline pilot. The third one is in the insurance business not far from here. It really is wonderful not to have to worry about them.

J. Did you look up your exwife?

S. No, well, she happens to live in the same town my boy lives in, so I bought a couple of plants in Evanston while I was waiting for my boy to pick me up. I bought one for her and gave it to his wife to take over. But she [exwife] refused it. If she feels that way about it, all I could do was just make a gesture and that's the way it is.

115

J.   Are you thinking about writing up any of your experiences?

S.   Out in Chicago? No, there wasn't anything particularly eventful there. Oh, I didn't know what to do with myself in some of the hours that I had. I'd walk through Northwestern Station, which was just East of where I had all my early boyhood experiences. It was amazing how that section has been razed, practically completely. There's only a couple of buildings left and they're in the process of condemnation. And Halsted and Madison Street is going to be one of the extensions of the Loop area. A great big new Holiday Hotel is built there. The open land there is probably slated for highrises. I was very much surprised—it was like I was walking in a cemetery—all these old landmarks, all those old saloons—I didn't see one drunk on the street (laughs). Outside of that, I didn't find anything particularly interesting there. I was glad to get back. I felt like I was lost there.

22

On Being Mugged

Stanley I came home about one o'clock one morning and parked my car here in front of the house. I got out and looked around the car to see if everything was all right. All of a sudden a man ran toward me. It appeared strange—What was he running for at one o'clock in the morning? If I would have thought that there was something wrong, I would have gotten my shillelagh out of the car. It's pretty heavy, with a wooden handle—quite a lethal weapon. I just have it there in case of protection. Sometimes you never know what will happen.

So he ran into me and took me by surprise. He was pretty husky and his weight bowled me over and at the same time he flayed at me with his fists. He hit me in the face and knocked me down. I hit the curb, and that's when the hip bone was broken. He went through my pockets and shook me down. He didn't say a word. In my back pocket I keep my identification in my wallet. My money I always keep in my right-hand pocket. I had quite a bit of money in this pocket—over $500. I had my hand over this pocket just lightly so that he wouldn't feel the money. So he missed the money. In the meantime I'm howling like a stuck pig.

Sonia: I didn't hear it, I was in the back bedroom sound asleep.

S. So he ran down the street and it wasn't long before the paramedics came. The police questioned me and asked did I recognize the guy? "I wish I could," I says, "I'd get that sonofabitch." If I ever got that shillelagh I think I'd have killed him, I really would. He was a big fellow, and I don't like to be intimidated. If I could have gotten this weapon—not a weapon—just a little protection. So anyway, I went to the hospital and that's all there was to it. Nobody ever heard of this fellow again.

Jon What did he look like?

S. Well, he seemed to be a fellow about thirty years old, blond, well built. It was one o'clock in the morning; I didn't get a good look at him. It was a multiple fracture of the femur and also the hip.

I did think as I was lying there, "Well, this is just compensation" (laughing). I thought of what I did to others in my younger life. Perhaps I'm fatalistic.

J. Do you think this man saw you leaving the card place?

S. No, I thought about it later. You see, when you cash your chips in at Gardena you have to go to the window. People see the exchange. I won a few hundred dollars. So I might have been followed from Gardena, and they knew I had the money.

J. Did you see anybody at Gardena that was watching you?

S. No, I didn't notice anything. They don't have many unshady characters at Gardena. They weed those people out.

J. How long has it been?

S. October 15 [1978].

J. Almost two months ago?

S. Yeah. But taking all things into consideration, at my age, seventy-one, I'm lucky that I have recuperative powers.

I didn't like it, of course, lying in the hospital with a broken leg and thigh, but I just thought, "Well, it could have been a hell of a lot worse." He could have killed me, or put a knife to me. The money part is incidental, although I did have a sense of satisfaction that he didn't get a dime. If he knew there was $500 in my pocket (much laughter), he'd have been sick. He'd have been a lot sicker if I could have got to the car, believe me. I'd 've killed him. My fury would be so deep that by the time I'd got my senses, I'd have probably beaten his head in. On the other hand, I thought afterward, that's the way I was—that's what I did. What do I expect but some of the same treatment. I'm just as susceptible. Maybe I was harder on my victims. I remember one of the cases where we did pummel this guy pretty good. He was in court and his head was bandaged. He was in bad shape. So, *I* was brutal!

Part IV
Commentaries

23

The Jack-Roller:
The Appeal, the Person,
and the Impact

Gilbert Geis

Only a very few of the hundreds of sociological treatises published in 1930 remain in print today. *The Jack-Roller* is one of these unusual survivors. What is there about the book that accounts for its staying power? Does its vitality lie with the sociological insights that are implicit in Stanley's autobiographical writings and/or those explicitly set forth by the commentators, Clifford R. Shaw and Ernest W. Burgess? Or has the book endured beyond the usual alloted time span for its genre because it offers an interesting story that is well told? Or, as sometimes happens, has *The Jack-Roller* acquired an unmerited reputation for scholarly sagacity, a reputation that is not able to withstand close contemporary scrutiny? This chapter seeks to determine the appeal of *The Jack-Roller* and the impact on the study of juvenile delinquency, the academic subject to which it was addressed.

The Appeal

On a rather simple level, I suspect that its title has added considerably to the survival of *The Jack-Roller* (oddly, I do not find the word *jack-roller* in my unabridged dictionary). The title promises to provide an interesting tour of back-alley crime, though in truth the book's contents tell the reader very little about the craft and the perils of bashing and robbing drunken men at night on dark and dimly lit city streets. Publishers know the importance of titles and at times will rename a book to cater to what they suppose to be national buying tastes: note, for instance, how Hemingway's *Fiesta,* published in England, was *The Sun Also Rises* for the American market. It is significant that *The Natural History of a Delinquent Career* (1931) and *Brothers in Crime* (1938), both life stories put together by delinquents under Shaw's supervision, and both seemingly contributions at least as notable as *The Jack-Roller,* did not enjoy nearly the same in-print longevity as *The Jack-Roller.*

The book's history can hardly rest on so slim a reed, however. Much more important for the survival of *The Jack-Roller,* and for its elevation to the status of a sociological classic, is the story that Stanley tells. I am almost certain that the basic appeal that Stanley's life history contains, however, has very little to do with the matters emphasized by Shaw (and those stressed by Burgess in the epilogue). The ecological milieus are of mild interest when described by Stanley and of even lesser interest when analyzed by Shaw, who is not above padding a slim manuscript (only 205 printed pages) by telling us much more than we conceivably need to know about things such as an affluent zone (on the basis of the fact that Stanley had a brief period of residence there as a foster child).

Nor do matters of process, stressed by Shaw and Burgess, seem to be so absorbing or so novel. It hardly appears unusual or informative to have documented for us the growth in criminal sophistication of a youngster who is inexorably dedicated to violating the law because, as he sees things, such behavior and the persons involved in it with him are the most absorbing things that he can imagine. Perhaps such a process was eye-opening when *The Jack-Roller* first was published. If so, then the book unfortunately has suffered in retrospect from its very virtues, by becoming something so commonplace that it now appears trite. I rather doubt this; I think the book provides details about a specific instance of a reasonably well understood process of movement through stages of criminal involvement. Indeed, perhaps the most surprising aspect of Stanley's career in crime and delinquency is the absence of any progression into the ranks of the truly sophisticated and successful mobsters, despite a keen interest in participating in their activities. Yet this is a matter that draws no comment whatsoever from either Shaw or Burgess.

What stands out for me much more than either the ecological ideas or the points about process in *The Jack-Roller* is the relentless unveiling by Stanley of the horrors of the various facilities into which he was placed—the detention centers, jails, and reformatories. We know about the nature of life in penal institutions, those of us who read John Howard and Charles Dickens, though Stanley generously fuels his narrative with much more than a fair share of self-pity. Even so, Stanley draws particularly vivid portraits of the cruelty of many people and the awfulness of his confinements.

What I find puzzling is the apparent indifference on the part of both Shaw and Burgess to the institutional conditions portrayed by Stanley. Burgess seems to ignore the matter, focusing almost totally on his own astute, if rather pedantic highlights of Stanley's career, inventory of personality traits, and statement professing the value of personal histories. It seems obvious that Burgess's role for this volume is to help legitimate an approach that Shaw seems chronically ill at ease about professionally, if I interpret correctly Shaw's constant sycophantic references to William Healy and W.I. Thomas. It is as if their imprimatur might establish satisfactorily the bona fides of the life history as a method of scientific work.

Shaw comments on institutional conditions in a pair of footnotes. One contains the exculpatory observation that "every effort is made to cope with the problem of sex perversion among the boys. At present an officer is placed on guard in the dormitory each night."[2] The other is the oddly dead-pan statement that "one of the most frequent complaints made by inmates in penal institutions is with reference to the monotonous character of the routine of prison life."[3]

Perhaps I am being unduly critical. Shaw may have thought it courageous to publish this unedited and stark exposé of prison life. On the basis of internal evidence in the book, however, I am inclined to believe that Shaw took rather lightly Stanley's depictions as if examples of his perceptual aberration. Also, Shaw and Burgess were so intent on their mission of analysis and treatment, looking for those meaningful "group associations," that they overlooked the terrible story of misery and malevolence that Stanley set before them.

The Person

To my mind the appeal of *The Jack-Roller* must be credited not to its sociological insights and contributions but to the extraordinary nature of Stanley himself. The protagonist is truly Dostoyevskian in his complexity and in his appalling ability to act in ways that seem stunningly self-destructive and self-defeating by almost anyone's standards. Stanley tells us that he cannot tolerate the smallest degree of monotony, that he cannot abide the "stares of snobbish people," and that he will not take reasonable orders especially if they are issued by a woman. In addition, Stanley describes how he is hooked and drawn, lemming-like, to the sordid and gaudy, Loop area of the city. We read, hardly believing his reports of blowing up emotionally, walking off jobs, and starting fights over trivial matters. Stanley seems to know precisely what he is doing, as he unselfconsciously recites his experience and is simultaneously presumably unaware of the likely consequences of his actions. There is something extremely perplexing in so forthcoming, guilt free and self-righteous a tale, with the teller able to state the connections between choice and consequence but obviously incapable of doing much about it.

I found it intriguing to meet with Stanley in his Los Angeles apartment a few years ago. It took no imagination to tie the contemporary man to the 1930s youngster. Stanley was a thoroughly charming man, neatly and finely dressed, and preternaturally concerned with my welfare. Yet in the course of the afternoon, he absolutely was immutable in regard to his perceptions about a world against which constant vigilance had to be exercised if one were not to be fooled or done in.

For example, he related a story about a barroom brawl, another telling of the Sunset Bar scene, (see chapter 20), which allowed me to put the question that had perplexed me while I read his autobiography. I asked how he could not see that his chip-on-the-shoulder attitude would inevitably impel him into conflict. He seemed at a loss to conceive of any other posture except one of feisty belligerence in the face of any possible slight. To back down, to turn aside, to adopt an ameliorative position was unthinkable. He did not say this, but he conveyed it clearly in his inability to grasp the possibilities of alternative responses. Stanley merely repeated the litany that began with the other person's actions and how he had responded with a counterattack: leaving the job, telling the woman off, or getting into the fight (it seemed especially if he was outclassed by a much younger man).

I appreciate that elements of this view of life attach much more to Stanley's social heritage that to mine, but I submit that Stanley, given his background, is nonetheless far from the norm. The queston of Stanley's intelligence provides an interesting illustration of this thesis. Healy's report based on testing at the Juvenile Psychopathic Institute states that Stanley is "very bright."[4] Shaw seems intent on regressing him toward the norm by maintaining several times that Stanley's intelligence was no better than "average."[5] This represents one of a number of the author's rather heavy-handed attempts to place an unusual case into the mainstream of delinquency, and thereby to render the study more prototypical than it otherwise might be.

However limited his repertoire of behaviors for dealing with real or imagined antagonisms, Stanley assuredly was more than disarmingly amiable during my brief visit. Perhaps it is only in certain unstructured situations, ones containing the prospect of threat, such as unemployment, divorce and abandonment, that compel Stanley to defend the territory in which his self-image is at stake.

Had I not met Stanley, I might have been more open to the idea that his story became an assignment set forth for Shaw's benefit. Very few individuals are glorified as case histories in scholarly circles at so young an age. It may have been tempting to play the role if the behavior was interesting enough to carry a book. However, the straightforward manner of Stanley in person convinced me of the authenticity of the attitudes expressed originally in *The Jack-Roller*.

In summary, I find *The Jack-Roller* relatively lightweight as a sociological contribution. The oft-repeated observation in the book that most vital are Stanley's perceptions, not their truth, seems to carry W.I. Thomas's catch phrase far beyond its real importance. Both fact and perceptions of fact are essential if we want better understanding, and it can be a feckless enterprise to proceed on the basis only of perceptions. It is telling that Shaw goes to considerable length to reassure us that he had checked carefully

Stanley's official biography, most notably, his offense record, but that he has no apparent interest in getting corroboration or refutation of Stanley's other material. How did his stepmother, his stepbrother, his partners, and others view the episodes that are described by Stanley, and how does Stanley affect other people? These are all vital matters if we aim at accurate and worthwhile interpretations. On the other hand, as Stanley reveals himself to us, I consider him a fascinating and frustrating human being, well worth attention as a literary autobiographical figure.

The Impact

The Jack-Roller derives its power as a psychological study, not as a document laying bare sociological ideas. Yet it has been heralded as the latter kind of contribution, presumably because it was written by a sociologist with a strong social work and social action bent and directed toward a sociological audience. The back-cover blurb of the 1966 Phoenix edition notes, with the hyperbole allowed such material, that *The Jack-Roller* "helped to establish the life-history or 'own story' as an important instrument of sociological research." Howard S. Becker pursues this theme in a thoughtfully and elegantly written foreword to this paperback issue of the book.

Becker wistfully notes that qualitative work like *The Jack-Roller* is in short supply and low repute in contemporary sociology. Life histories are considered by Becker to be more valuable than fiction in generating hypotheses and insights since they are not aimed at achieving esthetic and artistic goals (I wonder if this is true in regard to Stanley). Rather, they are responsive to sociological interrogation; that is, the writer can be asked to address issues of importance to the discipline.

I found Becker's proposition defensible but arguable. In contradiction, it can be said that by dictating the list of topics for the delinquent to address, the investigator selects the material to fit into his own biases about what is important. Becker also made a strong claim for the spontaneous value of life histories:

> To understand why someone behaves as he does you must understand how it looked to him, what he thought he had to contend with, what alternatives he saw open to him; you can only understand the effects of opportunity structures, delinquent subcultures, social norms, and other commonly invoked explanations of behavior by seeing them from the actor's point of view.[6]

Becker, all told, puts forward a decent case for the scientific importance of the life history as a superior or at least a supplementary method for learning about social behavior in its complexity; a method not truncated by the rigidities of quantitative constructs that also permits the unfolding of the variegated drama that marks social existence. Becker's comments, however, are more of an elegy than an inspiration, and "the boy's own story," in Shaw's Dodsworthian phrase, had a brief stay and is only to be mourned. Shaw himself, with a pronounced defensiveness that pervades his commentary, seems to anticipate a declasse fate for the life history as a method of scientific research.

I will now assess this impact, first by examining the reviews of the book when it first appeared, and then by discussing its role in the literature on juvenile delinquency.

Reviews

I did not read the reviews of *The Jack-Roller* before I wrote the foregoing impressions because I wanted my response to the book to remain uncontaminated by what others had said about it when it was first published. However admirable the intent, my exercise in self-restraint largely was unnecessary. Nine reviewers wrote laudatory pro forma recountings of the contents of the book (much taken with detailing Stanley's delinquencies and crimes) and concluding with delight that Stanley had settled into law-abiding ways.

A review by Kimball Young, however, was an exceptional one that I found to be most valuable. Young commented, as I had, on Burgess's analysis, calling it "brilliant."[7] (I had found it "astute," and I am not much given to praise.) Young then put forward a very important point that I had overlooked, noting that Burgess had emphasized the "interplay of certain temperamental traits with social and cultural conditioning" in explaining Stanley's life course. Simply put, Burgess was proclaiming that Stanley's youthful traits were assuredly "givens," but what direction they would lead him in depended ultimately on the social situation in which he found himself. Burgess's observation is set, of course, into the mainstream of sociological thought of that time and, though to a lesser extent, of today as well. I believe that it is for the most part incorrect, at least if taken very far or very literally. Indeed, Burgess's interpretation points to a key lesson that can be drawn from the fact that we now have available a follow-up study of Stanley covering the half century since *The Jack-Roller* was put together.

I believe, given his outlook, that Stanley was destined to get into many kinds of difficulties regardless of his surroundings and status—at least to the extent that he operated in the social context of this society and that he interacted with other persons. I do not mean to press a theorem of inexorable linkage between what we are at any point and what happens to us later, but merely to take exception to that heavy-handed sociological commitment to the view that social conditions totally can reshape and redefine all behavior. Statistical regularities appertain to personality configurations, however wobbly and uncertain at time such relationships may appear and however hopeless it often may be to try to predict the outcome in regard to any particular person. This is true especially if that person tends to be amorphously located somewhere in the 20 to 80 percent range in terms of behavioral and personality patterns. But there are things that can be said about the likely consequences of established patterns that, it seems to me, stand a very good chance of being accurate. That Stanley would enjoy less than normally smooth or more than normally uneven relationships with women, for example, seems to be a rather predictable outcome that neither a job as a salesman nor marriage to a saint was likely to alter.

Kimball Young as did virtually all the reviewers, reveled a bit in the seeming happy resolution of Stanley's early troubles, pointing in his review to the jack-roller's "final reorientation to normal social participation."[8] The reviewer for the *New York Times* marked as well the "treatment which apparently has ended in the boy's complete redemption,"[9] while T.V.S. (probably T.V. Smith, a well-known social philosopher of the time) in the *International Journal of Ethics* noted that Stanley had become a "socially oriented person on the road to conventional success."[10] Read Bain thought it "almost unbelievable" that a combination of Shaw and a loving landlady, the anonymous Mrs. Smith, "could snatch the brand from the burning."[11] Indeed, the *Christian Century* was so taken with Stanley's redemption that it headnoted its review "A Modern Prodigal's Return," and observed in its text that "for the past five years [Stanley] has been going pretty straight . . . [and] is an adjusted member of society and no longer an enemy of it or an irresponsible drifter on its surface."[12] It appears singular that Stanley's alleged reformation, only one element in the book, preoccupied the reviewers. Perhaps Shaw sensed that the final reckoning hardly was in, so he downplayed this item vis-à-vis the reviewers, who liked the upbeat denouement of the tale, however uncertain they must have known it to be.

Only the *London Times Literary Supplement* focused on Stanley's personality to the extent that I did in my earlier observations. Its unnamed reviewer found the book to be "in many ways a characteristic product of modern American sociological research," a cryptic remark that got no further explication. Stanley was called "vainglorious," "unctuous," "pronouncedly egocentric," and marked by "complacency."[13] I take this to be in some measure an English reaction to what culturally would be regarded as alien forms of self-expression on Stanley's part, especially since the British reviewer merely conveys his considerable distaste regarding such traits, and makes no attempt to tie them to the chronicle under review.

Bain has the only critical observation regarding the methodology, suggesting that Stanley's obvious "literary ability" might well indicate that he was not representative of the cadre of persons whose attitudes and actions might be more accurately taken to characterize juvenile delinquents. This possible methodological inadequacy of *The Jack-Roller* was more severly dealt with by Edwin H. Sutherland then at the University of Chicago, in a later review of Shaw's *The Natural History of a Delinquent Career.* Sutherland, as I did, took exception to the point that the guidance of the sociologist-commentator would make the life history particularly pertinent to sociological concerns. "The procedure," Sutherland noted, "is likely to result in some selection of material in a sense that the relative amounts of material on different topics are influenced by the interests and hypotheses of the investigator." As an illustration, Sutherland suggested that the reading of the diverse case histories published by Shaw conveys the impression that the family and neighborhood are "immensely important in the formation of delinquent careers and that the broader culture and social organization are relatively unimportant, at least in a direct manner." Such a conclusion, Sutherland noted, might be correct, but it also "may be the result of the methodology used in such case studies."[14]

It remained for Kimball Young, himself something of an iconoclast, to offer the only mild critique of the ideology that pervaded Shaw's case history materials as set forth in *The Jack-Roller*:

> This is an instance of the reformation of a person by removing him from the causal situation. It is not the outcome of any modification of the precipatating condition itself. Nothing is done to improve the nature of the life of people residing in the slum and delinquency areas out of which Stanley came. The major social problem still remains. One asks why no more adequate provision is made for playgrounds, for socially-approved means of extraschool education, for all those institutional formulations which would remove the major causes of such behavior: illness, low standards of living, unemployment, and all the rest.[15]

Textbooks and Monographs

Any contributor to the literature of social science who slyly or otherwise glances at footnotes and peruses texts to try to determine an individual's "impact" upon a scholarly field learns how treacherous such an endeavor is apt to be. Stray platitudes and subordinate themes often wend their way into productions as if representative of a person's thinking. "Fame," the legal scholar Edmond Cahn once observed, is "one's name recognized while one's thought is ignored" and involves "misapprehensions grosser and more offensive than the most malevolent insults." He added: "Fame has a bangle at hand to aid in her fraud; it is the seductive illusion that posterity will display more intelligent taste and discrimination than one's contemporaries—an illusion which in most cases posterity can be trusted to refute."[16]

The subtleties of scholarly citation remain almost totally unexamined. What we have to date are crude counts of references that are taken as a rough index of impact and influence. The number of citations are, of course, highly dependent on factors peripheral to the value of a contribution. To mention but one example, works that are provacatively wrong minded may be cited to provide a springboard for a proper discussion of the topic. Indeed, it might be argued that the most effective way to command attention in the social sciences is to take an absolutely outré stance on an important disciplinary issue.

I undertook a qualitative review to try to obtain some sense of how later writers have come to regard and employ the materials found in *The Jack-Roller*. I checked the *Social Science Citation Index* in quest of information on journal attention to the book since 1960, the date to which the *Index* goes back. Then I sampled the university library and my own books (in the event that the best materials might be out on loan at the university). I looked at approximately sixty volumes that referred to *The Jack-Roller* before I decided that I had found satisfactory answers to my questions. The following are some of my conclusions:

1. Clifford Shaw remains one of the most heavily cited authors in the field of juvenile delinquency, despite the almost half century that has elapsed since his materials were published. Shaw is apt to be referenced many times in any juvenile delinquency textbook of today and yesteryear, and his work often is referred to in treatises on diverse aspects of the subject.

2. *The Jack-Roller* is not one of Shaw's works that receives the larger amount of attention from later writers. Shaw is regularly credited with discovering the fact that youngsters commit crimes in groups rather than alone. In addition, his conclusions on the relationship between broken homes and delinquency, his areal patterning of the phenomenon of delinquency, and his Chicago Area Project, a community action program, are accorded particular attention by later writers.

3. An extensive analytical review of Shaw's work is found in a monograph by Harold Finestone, an alumnus of the staff of the Institute for Juvenile Research, and a man who knew Shaw personally. Finestone maintains that on the subject of juvenile delinquency "almost every major subsequent development in research, theory, and practice elaborates on themes they [Shaw and his coworker Henry D. McKay] first explored." But Finestone is critical of Shaw's failure to make theoretical usage of case studies such as *The Jack-Roller*, and he points to "inconsistencies" between Shaw's analytical stress on "symbolic interaction," a social-psychological approach fashionable at the time among University of Chicago sociologists, and the emphasis in the case-study materials on cultural determinants of

behavior. Finestone also notes a "fatalistic" motif inherent in Shaw's reading of his case histories of delinquents.[17]

Finestones's work, is a special attempt to place Shaw into a intellectual context in regard to the study of juvenile delinquency and is not a direct representation of the impact of Shaw's work. The point that all subsequent developments in juvenile-delinquency scholarship play off Shaw's materials is accurate only in the sense that any theme is apt to be locatable in a body of work such as the life histories. Finestone's observation is overgenerous about Shaw's general influence.

4. A number of discussions of the life history as a research weapon in the social-science arsenal have also attended to *The Jack-Roller*, most notably contributions by Stuart Rice and John Dollard.[18] Dollard calls attention to a point made earlier, Stanley's failure to achieve overmuch in the criminal world, and claims that "we can only assume that this limitation of accessibility to the highest values of the criminal world was due to personality difficulties of his [Stanley's] own, not adequately specified in his autobiography."[19] Dollard's analysis may be taken as a generic critique of the life-history method for its tendency to be unresponsive to questions that others besides the original commentator might find important and, more specifically, as an observation on the idiosyncratic nature of Stanley's career and its unrepresentativeness of the class it is meant to examine.

5. Article writers, at least since 1960, do not employ *The Jack-Roller* as a basis for hypotheses that are tested under field or laboratory conditions. There is no gainsaying, of course, that the themes of *The Jack-Roller* may have been absorbed into the intellectual fibers of scholars, beyond the point where the book will be footnoted, despite germinal influence: but I rather doubt that this is what has happened. Instead, I believe that the significant function of hypothesis formation, emphasized by Becker, has not taken place so far as *The Jack-Roller* is concerned.

The Jack-Roller rarely is cited in journal literature in contrast to its very considerable representation in texts and monographs. Nonetheless, the book has provided the basis for some important journal observations. Two of the four articles during the 1960 to 1966 period that refer to *The Jack-Roller* can be briefly noted as exemplars. John M. Martin and his colleagues smartly observe that Shaw did not "successfully link his form of structural analysis to a psychological view which considered significant differences among individuals." For Shaw, Martin and his collaborators note, "personality seemed to be essentially the subjective side of culture."[20]

Alan Cubbon, in an intriguing reexamination of the famous Hawthorne study, adverts to *The Jack-Roller* to demonstrate his point that the Yale research them studying workers at General Western's plant were so influenced by University of Chicago sociology that, in the manner of Shaw, it failed to attend in any meaningful manner to the realities of the outside world.

"Capone and corruption" marked Chicago during the period covered by *The Jack-Roller*, Cubbon observes, but no one would have known that from an examination of Shaw's observations on his case study.[21]

6. What reasonably might be regarded as the two major contributions to the literature on delinquency in current times—Albert K. Cohen's *Delinquent Boys* and *Delinquency and Opportunity* by Richard Cloward and Lloyd Ohlin—make some note of Shaw's case studies.[22] Cohen draws illustrations of "gratuitous hostility" on the part of delinquents from the materials, while Cloward and Ohlin maintain that *The Jack-Roller* provides an illustration of the linkage between delinquency and adult crime, a matter which by no means is one of the book's major motifs, presuming it can be said to support the point at all. Cloward and Ohlin maintain that *The Jack-Roller* and Shaw's other life histories fail to live up to their claim to be "complete" explanations of delinquency since, first, they tell "very little about the kinds of pressures that impinge upon the motivational systems of individuals leading to delinquent subcultures"[23] and, second, they tell "very little about why the result is a criminal life rather than some alternative deviant pattern.[24] I take it that what is meant here accords with Finestone's suggestion that Shaw did not attempt to draw theoretical implications from his work and that Cloward and Ohlin are taking him to task for not addressing matters that they believe to be essential elements of an adequate explanation of gang delinquency. It is notable, of course, that by and large Stanley was a bit of a loner, while the now-classical theoretical literature on delinquency focuses on gang behavior—a subject much more amenable to the tools of sociological analysis than is Stanley's story.

7. The textbook and monograph literature noting *The Jack-Roller* pays primary attention to the associational processes by which a person moves through the delinquent world and learns certain attitudes, values, and skills. This is certainly a major theme of the book, though not the only one, as Shaw had it fashioned. LaMar T. Empey, for instance, offers quotations from *The Jack-Roller* to illustrate associational influences in delinquency: one tells of Stanley's interaction with "William;" another testifies to involvement with a girl delinquent; while a third portrays street behavior. Empey notes in passing that the usefulness of the life stories could be enhanced today by the addition of a historical perspective that outlined the social forces that created the conditions described in the autobiography.[25]

Muzafer and Carolyn Sherif, a preeminent team of social psychologists, also often employ Shaw's material to illustrate social processes involved in human behavior. They are taken with Stanley's fleeing from his well-to-do foster home to rejoin his Loop comrades, a matter that the Sherifs generalize as a process of "self-sacrifice in the interest of group solidarity."[26]

8. Matters other than process are less significant in the later attention paid to *The Jack-Roller*, though two recurrent points might be noted. There

is a rather common remark about the fact that Stanley's stepmother condoned his stealing,[27] while several writers use descriptions by Stanley of institutional conditions to buttress their own condemnation of facilities for delinquents.[28]

9. Equally as interesting as the matters that tend to be cited are those that are ignored. Only Martin Neumeyer, among the writers I examined, thought it worth noting that Stanley had been reformed.[29] Neumeyer, it may be remembered, was an earlier-generation scholar much in the mold of the Christian reformers who wrote several of the book reviews of *The Jack-Roller*. No reference, beyond Barron's, commented on the value of the life history for treatment purposes, a matter that dominated the book.

Milton L. Barron suggests in his juvenile-delinquency textbook that the "life history has long proved its value . . . not only for research into the factors 'causing' delinquent behavior, but also for the practical purposes of treatment."[30] It is a lovely sentiment, which Shaw assuredly would have appreciated since it states what he had hoped his book might accomplish. Unfortunately, the truth appears to be otherwise. *The Jack-Roller* does not seem to have exercised much obvious and direct influence on the literature of juvenile delinquency, at least in terms of references to it put forward to maintain particular positions or theories. Quantitative studies of juvenile delinquency offer much more substantial and lasting contributions to the corpus of information that is regarded as the basic body of data on the subject. This includes quantitative work by Shaw himself in contrast to the life histories he published. Much more, however, might have been expected from the life story, and it is to this lack of impact that I want to devote my concluding remark.

When Clifford R. Shaw embarked on a demonstration of the life history as a sociological research method and an advocacy of its extended use for causal theory and correction, he overlooked one fundamental and very simple point: *Stanley's story is interesting precisely because it is atypical.* One must generate life histories that are diverse if they are not to be redundant, and this cannot be done, and at the same time, proclaim representativeness (unless you extend considerably the milieu or age range covered). As Shaw chose to employ it with delinquents, the life-history technique was severely self-limiting and, in truth, Shaw's work very quickly eroded the vein it set out to explore. Eighty-five case histories are said to remain in the Shaw-McKay archives, and there is no clamor to see them into print because they offer very little that is new and much that is repetitive. To keep this genre vital, Shaw would have had to discover "different" kinds of delinquents, whose difference in some telling way would additively enhance our understanding of the general phenomenon. It is a formidable task, well beyond Shaw's interest and perhaps beyond the capacity of our discipline. *The Jack-Roller*, both the original and the sequel in this volume, provide an object lesson in some of the strengths and pitfalls of such an enterprise and pose a great challenge to others to revivify life-history work.

Notes

1. Clifford R. Shaw, *The Jack-Roller: A Delinquent Boy's Own Story*, 2nd ed. (Chicago: University of Chicago Press, 1966) pp. 39-40. All quotations in this chapter reprinted from *The Jack-Roller: A Delinquent Boy's Own Story* by Clifford R. Shaw are by permission of the University of Chicago Press, copyright © 1930 by The University of Chicago, Introduction copyright © 1966 by The University of Chicago.

2. Ibid., p. 69.

3. Ibid., p. 155.

4. Ibid., p. 190.

5. Ibid., p. 24.

6. Ibid., p. vii.

7. Reprinted from review of *The Jack-Roller* by Kimball Young, in the *American Journal of Sociology* 36 (November 1930):474, by permission of The University of Chicago Press. Copyright © 1930 by The University of Chicago.

8. Ibid.

9. *New York Times*, review of *The Jack-Roller,* 21 December 1930, p. 20.

10. T.V.S., Review of *The Jack-Roller, International Journal of Ethics* 41(October 1930):128.

11. Read Bain, review of *The Jack-Roller, Annals of the American Academy of Political and Social Science* 51 (September 1930):285.

12. Winfred E. Garrison, review of *The Jack-Roller, Christian Century* 47 (25 June 1930):818.

13. *London Times Literary Supplement*, review of *The Jack-Roller*, 28 August 1930, p. 678.

14. Edwin H. Sutherland, review of *The Natural History of A Delinquent Career, American Journal of Sociology* 38 (July 1932):136.

15. Young, review of *The Jack-Roller,* p. 476.

16. Edmond Cahn, *The Moral Decision* (Bloomington: Indiana University Press, 1959) p. 203.

17. Harold Finestone, *Victims of Change: Juvenile Delinquents in American Society* (Westport, Connecticut: Greenwood, 1976), p. 77.

18. Stuart A. Rice, ed., "Hypotheses and Verifications in Clifford R. Shaw's Studies of Juvenile Delinquency," in *Methods in Social Science: A Case Book* (Chicago: University of Chicago Press, 1931); and John Dollard, *Criteria for the Life History* (New Haven: Yale University Press, 1935).

19. Dollard, *Criteria for the Life History*, p. 193.

20. John M. Martin, Robert E. Gould, and Joseph P. Fitzpatrick, "Delinquency in its Community Context," *Social Service Review* 42 (September 1965):327.

21. Alan Cubbon, "Hawthorne Talk in Context," *Occupational Psychology*, vol. 43, (1969):111-128.

22. Albert K. Cohen, *Deinquent Boys: The Culture of the Gang* (New York: The Free Press, 1955); and Richard A. Cloward and Lloyd E. Ohlin, *Delinquency and Opportunity: A Theory of Delinquent Gangs* (New York: Free Press, 1960).

23. Cloward and Ohlin, *Delinquency and Opportunity*, p. 22.

24. Ibid, p., 36,

25. LaMar T. Empey, *Juvenile Delinquency: Its Meaning and Construction* (Homewood, Illinois: Dorsey, 1978).

26. Muzafer and Carolyn W. Sherif, *An Outline of Social Psychology*, rev. ed. (New York: Harper, 1956), p. 156.

27. Martin H. Neumeyer, *Juvenile Delinquency in Modern Society*, 3rd ed. (Princeton: D. Van Nostrand, 1961), p. 182; Martin R. Haskel and Lewis Yablonsky, *Juvenile Deliquency* (Chicago: Rand McNally, 1974), p. 110; and Herbert A. Block and Frank T. Flynn, *Delinquency: The Juvenile Offender in America Today* (New York: Random House, 1956), p. 174.

28. Negley K. Teeters and John O. Reinemann, *The Challenge of Delinquency* (New York: Prentice Hall, 1950), p. 463; Pauline V. Young, *Social Treatment in Probation and Delinquency* (New York: McGraw Hill, 1937), p. 209; and John R. Ellingston, *Protecting Our Children from Criminal Careers* (New York: Prentice Hall, 1948), p. 89.

29. Neumeyer, *Juvenile Delinquency in Modern Society*, p. 184.

30. Milton L. Barron, *The Juvenile in Delinquent Society* (New York: Knopf, 1956), p. 88.

References

Shaw, Clifford R. 1931. *The Natural History of a Delinquent Career*. Chicago: University of Chicago Press.
————. 1938. *Brothers in Crime*. Chicago: University of Chicago Press.

24

Life History, Autobiography, and the Life Cycle

James F. Short, Jr.

In his introduction to the 1966 reissue of *The Jack-Roller*, Howard Becker notes that the autobiographer "is telling us only part of the story, that he has selected material so as to present us with the picture of himself he would prefer us to have and that he may have ignored what would be trivial or distasteful to him, though of great interest to us."[1] *The Jack-Roller at Seventy* is more an autobiography than a life history, despite editor Jon Snodgrass's attempts to achieve chronology and emphasis on personal experience in the narrative and secure elaboration of some points. The autobiography lacks the advantage, for social-science purposes, of supplementation by case material of the sort gathered by Clifford R. Shaw to corroborate and place in context the earlier life history. It is more difficult, in this second account, to identify "rationalizations, fabrications, prejudices, (and) exaggerations,"[2] and to separate them from the perceptions of others, and to place them in context, as Shaw attempted to do in the earlier study. The success of Shaw's attempts to bring objectivity to life histories and explore the behavioral context were matters of debate following publication of *The Jack-Roller* and the other books in the series of life histories.[3] The observation that the autobiographer tells "only part of the story" should not be taken as criticism unique to autobiography since no one or no method can "tell the full story." Different methods tell different parts of the story and tell them differently. Life history, as practiced by Shaw, was more comprehensive and used more methods to discover "the story" than does the present document.

The present study has a second, equally important, disadvantage for social-science purposes: it is not part of a common enterprise such as that which was shared by the many early Chicago studies. *The Jack-Roller* and the other studies carried out by Shaw, McKay, and their collaborators at the Illinois Institute for Juvenile Research were a product of the vision shared by many in the flowering of the Chicago School of Urban Sociology. That vision was the advancement of an empirical science of sociology—indeed of the social sciences—with the city as its laboratory.[4] The enthusiasm accompanying the enterprise has been described by Faris as an "atmosphere . . . of adventure, exploration, and responsibility for opening up new directions of sociological research."[5] One result of the numerous studies in this flowering was that, as Becker remarks, "The contribution of any study could . . . be evaluated in the context of the total enterprise, not as though it stood alone.''[6] The story of Stanley's early life was embedded in the Chicago School of Urban Sociology in its rich stock of local knowledge as well as in the emerging science of sociology that the Chicagoans envisioned.

There is no fund of specialized local knowledge to which we can relate Stanley's later life. Contemporary social science does not encourage the multifaceted study of the community that characterized the Chicago School.[7] But this great strength of the Chicago School was also a source of limitation even then, inasmuch as the forces that shape people's lives—and greatly influence communities—extend beyond the community. Stanley's later life took him to several cities and a succession of jobs, incarcerations, and personal relationships. His adult years spanned a great depression, a world war and other wars, a tumultuous period of civil-rights activity in this country, revolutions in science, and momentous social changes in many parts of the world.

What, then, can we learn from Stanley's later story? We still can learn a good deal about how this particular individual defined situations and how he responded to them. We can discover important aspects of how this man defined himself, and his life. Insofar as the latter story indicates continuity with the earlier life history in important respects, we can have some confidence in the veracity of Stanley's account of his beliefs, attitudes, and behavior. Paraphrasing Becker, we can begin to ask questions about life from the point of view of a particular life. We also can interpret Stanley's account of his life from the perspective of other research, and interpretations from other studies can be compared with what Stanley has told us.

It appears, for example, that Stanley was little concerned with many larger events and forces that were shaping the world of his time. Larger forces and events are, of course, consequential for all, no matter how aware or concerned we are about them. Stanley's story is in no small measure the story of a life lived during periods of depression, war, and rapid social change. Most of his occasional comments on the Great Depression, on labor unions and governmental policy, for example, are in the nature of social commentary and philosophy of life rather than accounts of personal experience. That philosophy of life included deep loyalty to this country and acceptance of its economic system, in spite of his disappointing experiences under that system. It also embraced very traditional values with respect to sex roles, family life, and interpersonal relationships. It is characteristic of Stanley, in adulthood as in adolescence, that he personalizes his problems rather than viewing them in systemic terms. Yet his narrative is not as revealing of personal experience as we might wish.

To some exent the personal-problem focus of this story may be a function of the necessary limitations of space and investigator interest, and especially in the earlier life history, in which Stanley was asked to talk about his life, guided by his record of police contacts, court appearances, and incarcerations. Stanley was very much aware of the earlier book and his early and later relationships with Shaw, as both he and Jon Snodgrass make clear. While the narrative is relatively free of constraints as to content, the editor's questions and identity as a criminologist perhaps oriented Stanley to focus on and interpret his personal problems and behaviors. Despite a brief fling at politics in the 1930s, a "philosophical commentary," and a reference to disappointment at being rejected for service in World War II, Stanley evidences little interest in ongoing events in the larger society. This is hardly surprising in view of his constant struggle for economic sustenance and personal freedom, his concern for his children, and the lack of stability in his personal life as a result of incarceration, marital problems, and personality characteristics.

On Delinquent Behavior, Labeling, and Rehabilitation

We know very little about the later lives of juvenile delinquents. The statistics of recidivism, self-reports of delinquent and criminal behavior, and victimization surveys necessarily gloss over much of the personal and situational nature of the behavior under scrutiny. Oral history can inform us on such matters, but we are reminded that "as the past lengthens, its influence on the present (and future) becomes more difficult to assess."[8]

At this juncture in the history of social science, Stanley's autobiography, if it is to be useful, must go beyond "illustration of method" and "a basis for formulating tentative hypotheses" as Shaw suggested were its chief contributions. Despite limitations of the single case and the idiosyncratic nature of this very personal document, Stanley's story bears on some of those "tentative hypotheses," and social policies that have been advanced since the appearance of the original work. Shaw's caution "against drawing conclusions regarding the causes of delinquency or the relative merits of different methods of treatment upon the basis of this single case record" remains a warning against too easy generalization, however.[9]

Stanley's later story has little to do with delinquency, but his delinquent behavior and related experiences bear importantly on his later life. His early family life and economic circumstances and his involvement with various institutional authorities and especially with Shaw were important to his adult life. His early record and *The Jack-Roller* followed him for much of his adult life, particularly while he was living in Chicago. His adult life was complicated enormously by his later incarceration in a mental hospital. Surely the prognosis, in view of these circumstances, was bleak for any sort of "normal" adjustment.

Stanley's reactions to his earlier incarcerations, and the reactions of others, informed the labeling perspective that emerged twenty years after *The Jack-Roller* was published. His experiences with the juvenile justice system and institutional authorities were pervasive throughout his childhood. His sense of drama and its portrayal were hallmarks of the earlier story. Even then it was clear that Stanley was not a passive recipient of labels imposed by virtue of his record of delinquency and his incarcerations. While he played the role of "old timer" and "hard-boiled gunman of wide experience" when he was sent to the reformatory at St. Charles for a second time, the delinquent role appears to have been a device for impressing his fellow prisoners more than a fundamental part of his self-concept. Despite his statement that he "wanted to get ahead in a criminal life, instead of being good," when he was paroled he worked for a time before running away and turning to begging and stealing because his parole violation made legitimate employment extremely risky.[10] Later, after more criminal involvement, incarcerations, exposure to more sophisticated criminals and an expression of despair that "there was no hope but in crime,"[11] Stanley tells us in this volume that "no allure remained to resume a career of crime."[12] It was perhaps at this point that his relationship with Shaw became crucial.

By the customary criteria, Stanley recidivated well after initiation of Shaw's treatment program. He did so, however, following repeated attempts to "make it" legitimately and in desperation as a result of strained economic circumstances. Two subsequent periods of forced confinement in a state mental hospital apparently had less impact on his self-conception than did earlier contacts with the juvenile justice system, for he steadfastly refused to accept the judgment that he was mentally ill. As was the case in some of his previous incarcerations for delinquency, he twice escaped from the mental hospital and proceeded to seek and find legitimate employment. Following the second escape, during which he and his partner stole an automobile, by his own account, he was able to avoid further incarceration. That he was able to do so, despite his previous history, and his involvement in a series of marginal jobs—as dishwasher, gandy dancer, bar tender, clean-up man, card dealer, and salesman—is a testament to his perseverance and determination not to spend more of his life in confinement.

Stanley's later life suggests the wisdom of "judicious non-intervention," urged by Lemert and others with respect to juvenile misbehavior,[13] and of Egon Bittner's warning that "professional solutions for all problems threaten to change our lives from the kind of haphazard, make-do, minding-one's-own-business kind of affairs it still is, to a smooth-running, scientifically rationalized consumer function."[14] Stanley's life never "ran smooth," yet he was able for most of his adult life to support himself, and he remained a caring human being—for family and friends—despite an inability to maintain stable, close relationships throughout his life. Given all that happened to Stanley after his adolescence, speculation as to the success or failure of Shaw's treatment program should be undertaken with extreme caution. As Bennett remarks, "Stanley does rot seem to be a failure, or a failure of Shaw's,"[15] since he did not follow the career in crime which surely would have been predicted on the basis of his extensive, and progressively more serious, involvement in delinquent behavior.

The popular support of "judicious nonintervention" by the juvenile justice system, has emphasized the latter word in the phrase (see, for example, Schur 1973). Yet, as critics of "radical nonintervention" have been quick to point out, the problems in the past that led to intervention cannot be made to go away by a "legislative slight-of-hand."[16] By any criterion, Stanley's early behavior would have called for some type of intervention. Healy recommended placement in a foster home when Stanley was less than eight years old,[17] and Shaw concurred.[18] We cannot know the effect of this type of early intervention. Shaw's later intervention, after Stanley had accumulated an astounding record, seems critical to his subsequent adjustment, however unsatisfactory that adjustment may be by some criteria. His somewhat marginal existence after *The Jack-Roller* was published seems a combination of many factors, not the least of which may have been his success in avoiding further incarceration following his second escape from the mental institution. Stanley's life, if nothing else, surely is a triumph of self-reliance over institutionalization and other forms of enforced treatment. Shaw's intervention had something to do with this accomplishment.

Bennett notes that "Shaw realized that former delinquents often remain marginal characters, such as Stanley has been."[19] For that matter, Kobrin points out Shaw's recognition that local community leaders did not always conform to "philistine specifications of respectability." (The Area Project was criticized for this fact,[20] but Shaw remained steadfast, however, in support of the principles of "local autonomy and organization, self-help and self-determination."[21]) Stanley's marginality is evident in many ways—in his occupational history, family history, recreational pursuits, and personal relationships. The fact that he is articulate and often reflective concerning these matters facilitates the "conversation between the classes," an important function of social science, as Reisman, Becker, and Bennett all note.

That conversation is enhanced, in Stanley's case, by his awareness of the social and cultural gaps between himself and others; for example, the various people with whom he came into contact as well as those who attempted to rehabilitate him. Families to which he was paroled, employers, chance acquaintances, and especially Shaw stand out in the narrative. His references to "the pleasant company of these two cultured people (Shaw and Leonard Cottrell) early in the present narrative sounds a major theme of his life—the contrast he sees in his own existence and a better, more refined life. For even in childhood, Stanley was impressed with the fact that others were better off than he, economically and remarks often on their greater social sophistication. His reading is directed in part to understand ing "how other people lived" and, one suspects, toward achieving a measure of refinement in his own.

Autobiography and the Life Cycle

Such theoretical implications as follow from Stanley's later story relate less to delinquency than to adult socialization and the life cycle, both growing interests among behavioral scientists.[22] This autobiography will not sustain analysis in depth at any level of explanation: individual, micro- or macrosociological. Too much is left out—years of time, areas of life—circumstances, thoughts, and behavior. An outline of his life, as Stanley perceives and presents it, is sketched, however, embellished by details he chooses to insert.

Clifford R. Shaw's first footnote commentary notes "Stanley's self-justificatory attitude toward his own problems and situations."[23] In his discussion, Burgess characterizes Stanley as a "self-defender" and inventories personality traits that he believes to be "attributes of the personality pattern of an individual who is able even under adverse circumstances to maintain his ego against an unfriendly and even hostile social world."[24] With only slight modification, Burgess's analysis holds up well in the light of the present document. Stanley's "sense of injustice," much in evidence in The Jack-Roller, is reinforced by perceptions of his wife's unfaithfulness and the perfidy of employers and friends. He continues to exhibit traces of other characterisitics in Burgess's inventory: self-pity, blaming and suspicion of others, superficial and fragile personal relationships, absorption in his own ideas and plans, resistance to influence from others, and self-rationalization. He remains given to moralization and to quick and strong reactions in many situations.

These persistent characteristics impress us more in Stanley's account of his life than do any apparent changes. His personality appears relatively fixed, as Burgess suggested was the case in The Jack-Roller. Clearly, however, Stanley changed in adulthood in important ways, and he appears to have gained insight into his "inability to adjust" and his inflexibility in dealing with others.[25] He is able apparently to appreciate his stepmother's burdens and he attributes less base motives to her than he did earlier. From the vantage point of old age he appears more content with both his past and present life than was the case during the earlier periods.

This measure of insight does not appear to have affected at least one of Stanley's chief behavior characteristics, however. He continues to react spontaneously to perceived affronts and exhibit the feistiness that marked his relationships with others all along. This personal quality, together with other recurring themes in *The Jack-Roller* and in this book, seems especially important in interpreting Stanley's life course. Themes that stand out include a pervasive sense of loneliness and a deeply felt need for close emotional ties. Loneliness for Stanley is both a result of interpersonal difficulties and a choice at times arising out of consideration for the possible embarrassment to others over "the mediocre performance my life."[26] Stanley's concern reminds us again of his early discomfort in the presence of those who were better off or more cultured than he, and again of the conversation between the classes. His extensive reading, one senses, is a genuine effort to learn and impress us with how far he has come from his early station in life. For whatever reasons, loneliness is an ubiquitous feature of his life. He cuts himself off from many relationships, yet expresses a "hunger for motherly care" and regret over his lonely existence.[27]

Recent life-cycle literature, informed by role theory and much additional research, contains suggestions that may be relevant both to Stanley's childhood and his later life, particularly with respect to his relationships with others. Brim has noted that "what is learned in socialization, is interpersonal relationships . . . much of personality is learned interpersonal relations. . . ."[28] And Weinstein lays particular stress on the importance of "acquiring the interpersonal skills—necessary to engage" in "extensive and quite subtle negotiations with others whose purposes are not complimentary to ours."[29] Stanley was reasonably successful in this respect as a salesman. Yet apparently he was unable to transfer such skills to other roles. "The ability to move easily from one role to another and to adjust rapidly to new situations," we noted in describing the "social disabilities" of the gang boys we studied in Chicago, "is a much cultivated art in modern urban society, particularly among upwardly mobile persons."[30] Like our gang boys, Stanley had great difficulty when he was "out of his element" socially. Unlike many of them, Stanley was not lacking in intelligence.[31]

In our attempt to account for the lack of social assurance and other social disabilities of our gang boys, we drew on early family relationships and later experiences in school (largely unsatisfactory, from the standpoint of both the school and the boys):

The two areas of experience ("the narrow range of their social experience within as well as outside the family") are mutually reinforcing in this respect. The family does not equip the child with the role-playing facility adequate to the demands of such institutions as the school, and unsatisfactory experiences in school further narrow the range of role-playing opportunities which later facilitate job success—"getting along" with employers and fellow workers, and more than this, "getting along" in new and strange situations generally.[32]

Weinstein offers a further insight into the development of interpersonal competence that may be particularly appropriate to understanding Stanley's problems in this respect. "Rigidity," he notes, "is an orientation interfering with interpersonal competence."[33] Rigidity was a major problem for Stanley throughout his adult life. This characteristic and its antecedents are less clear in his childhood, though it would not be surprising to find the development of somewhat rigid personal characteristics as a defense against trials and tribulations such as Stanley experienced early in life.

In any case, *later maturity*, Ernest Burgess's euphemism for old age (a term he preferred "for personal reasons" when I first met him in 1947) appears to have brought some measure of relief to Stanley from earlier pressures related to his deeply held views concerning sex roles and self-sufficiency and his problems with authority relationships of all types. Though he still chafes under perceived obligations related to expenditures on his behalf by his second wife, he appears less restless, somewhat less rigid, more accepting under present circumstances than at any earlier period. Even now, however, a cautious interpretation is in order because of the precarious nature of such self-appraisals. Stanley's assessment of his situation at the close of *The Jack-Roller*, four years after his release from the "house of corruption," also expressed contentment and optimism. Both documents thus reflect Stanley's construction of his *self-ontology*, a process common to all, suggests Hankiss: "Everyone builds his or her own theory about the history and course of his or her life by attempting to classify his or her particular successes and fortunes, gifts and choices, favorable and unfavorable elements of his or her fate according to a coherent, explanatory principle and to incorporate them within a historical unit."[34] We see the culmination of this process most clearly in this book in chapter 12.

At the time *The Jack-Roller* was written, Stanley could not foresee later problems in health, marriage, vocation, with authorities and in other interpersonal relationships. Many types of disruptions in his life—their frequency, variety, and severity—and Stanley's reactions to them, are among the more interesting and provocative features of the present document. In this respect, Stanley's life is suggestive for theories of adaptation to stress, particularly those that adopt a developmental perspective.

Lowenthal and Chiriboga note, in the research literature on adaptation to stress, that it is often difficult to determine what is stress and what is adaptation; and further, what are "causative, mediating, or outcome variables."[35] Stanley's life story epitomizes these difficulties and is characterized by a variety of stresses: the death of his mother when he was four, poverty, and a life "filled with sorrow and misery" attributed in large measure to "a no-good, ignorant, and selfish stepmother."[36] Experiences with authorities and institutions, resulting from repeated runaways and delinquent behaviors, were adaptive and stressful. Later-life experiences similarly cloud the distinction between stress and adaptation, for some doubtless represented adaptations to earlier stress while at the same time producing additional stress for Stanley.

Despite such difficulties, there may be clues to Stanley's behavior in this literature. In turn, his life may inform the life-course perspective on adaptation to stress. Socially, Stanley's rather marginal life-style and his frequently experienced and at times self-imposed social isolation quite probably result in part from early parental deprivation. Lowenthall and Chiriboga suggest that "such early loss of social support apparently generates extreme sensitivity and conflict about interpersonal relationships."[37] A life-style avoiding close involvements protects one from potential disappointments. Stanley's pattern of forming and breaking close relationships following the dissolution of his marriage appears to have been an adult adaptation of this sort. The close relationships that he did form, however, were extremely important to him, as evidenced by the fact that they bulk so large in the present reconstruction of his life.

The relationship between past and current life stress and adaptation is complex, and one should not succumb to the temptation to make too much of a single case, however tempting that may be. The most noteworthy feature of Stanley's life is the frequency with which he experienced stressful events and circumstances. The fact that he survived to old age is itself remarkable. That he did so suggests that both personal and situational elements must have been involved. The very rigidity in personal values and behavior that contributed to Stanley's problems earlier in life may well be a strength in old age, as "stability in the self concept" and "maintaining a sense of continuity, especially in the value system" become of increasing importance in adaptation to the aging process.[38] The intensity and variety of stress, during childhood, adolescence, and young adulthood may have increased his ability to survive in adulthood and, by comparison, to find a more lasting measure of contentment in old age. Lowenthal suggests that the "relativity of the appraisal of a circumstance as stressful" is important in determining its impact.[39] Stanley's "yardstick" of prior stress was a standard against which his relatively secure circumstances in later years must seem tranquil indeed. Even the marginality of his existence during extended periods of his life (for example, when he was an escapee from the mental institution, as a dealer in illegal card games, or living with a call girl) may have protected him from an even more accute self-perception of failure by conventional standards than would have been the case had he attempted to live solely by the prescriptions of those standards.

From the vantage point of age seventy—and that is the only vantage point from which we can learn very much about his life, since so much in earlier adult years remains unknown—Stanley appears in some respects not unlike Lowenthal's older men, a sample of mostly middle-class suburban

San Francisco men who were better educated and more successful, economically, than Stanley. Lowenthal describes these older men as less involved in sociopolitical affairs than the older women she studied, interested in avoiding the "hassles" that had characterized their lives in earlier periods,[40] not as anxious about financial security or the economic system as were the middle-aged men studied.[41]

Speculation beyond such fragments is hazardous. But Stanley's story can serve as a data point in the sociology, and perhaps the psychology, of the life course. As John Clausen notes, in his foreword to Glen Elder's "Children of the Great Depression:"

> We know that "life chances" depend on historical circumstances and on one's location in the social structure. But we are only beginning to formulate the nature of the linkages between particular kinds of experiences located in time and place, adaptive responses to these experiences, and long-term outcomes. Indeed, the great bulk of research on socialization influences simply assumes that particular patterns of relationship, guidance, or activity will influence later outcomes.[42]

Elder's "children" were born in 1920-1921. Stanley, who was born in 1907 thus falls in a cohort between these children and their parents. Stanley's cohort, in fact, may have been specially disadvantaged by the Great Depression. Thernstrom's study of five birth cohorts from Boston found that men born during the first decade of the twentieth century (Stanley's cohort) were less likely than men born earlier to achieve upward mobility from first to last job,[43] and higher proportions of men in this cohort "made no headway at all over their worklife."[44] This cohort effect is especially important to any comparison with persons in other cohorts in evaluating Stanley's occupational history.

Stanley also falls outside Elder's cohorts and others that have been studied most intensively in that his life lacked the family centeredness and relative stability in other ways that has characterized these studies.[45] Nevertheless it is clear that Stanley had great concern for his family, and his values relative to family life were quite traditional, as Elder found was the case among his deprived families. Only reluctantly did Stanley accept the necessity of his wife's employment outside the home, and he persuaded her to quite her job in 1939, when he felt able to assume the role of breadwinner. For Stanley the family appears to have served as an emotional haven from life's problems—one of many such havens he sought in the course of a lonely, emotionally deprived life. Lowenthal reports that early parental deprivation among some men (her "challenged group") is compensated for by "identities (forged) through work and other roles extending beyond the family," but that other stress types evidenced "a pronounced longing for intimacy."[46] We cannot locate Stanley precisely on Lowenthal's typology, but he appears to be neither overwhelmed nor self-defeating (Lowenthal's categories for those characterized, on one axis of her typology, as preoccupied with stressful events). In view of accumulated life stress (the other axis), therefore, Stanley would appear to fall among Lowenthal's "challenged." One is not quite certain just what Stanley's identity is, from the pages that follow, but it seems to involve his competence in sales and at cards, a somewhat macho image, and a nostalgia for past intimate associations in which Clifford R. Shaw continues to play an important role. Stanley appears to differ from Lowenthal's challenged older men in lacking strong current investment in close interpersonal relationships, though he continues to express his appreciation for such relationships in the past. We note, finally, in agreement with Lowenthal, et al., that Stanley's adjustment to old age appears to represent not so much a "disengaged" life-style (another familiar term in life-cycle analysis) "as a push to develop a more rewarding life . . . via a selective disengagement from nonrewarding involvements."[47]

Conclusion: Life-Course, Politics, and Some Personal Observations

The social distance between social scientists and those whom they study has been the object of much scrutiny and commentary. Editor Snodgrass has criticized Shaw, among others, for "ever-present reservations about the full endowment of the offender," for being sympathetic but not empathetic.[48] Yet Burgess emphasizes the necessity of empathy, rather than sympathy, as "the first step" toward establishing rapport and devising a course of treatment.[49]

Still, as Bennett notes, "moral evaluation will always limit appreciation of common humanity in oral histories of criminal offenders."[50] Shaw certainly was not given to moralizing about delinquent behavior or delinquents, though I agree with Bennett that "much of Shaw's thinking was based on acceptance of 'conventional values,' " and it was this, perhaps that made it more difficult for him to accept quite as easily or fully some forms of deviant behavior, such as drug addiction. I can recall Shaw's putdown of those who would feel or say, with reference to delinquents, "There but for the grace of God go I." Instead he would say, "There go I." While the point doubtless was made for dramatic effect, I have little doubt as to his sincerity.

In any case, it is well to note that Shaw as well as Stanley—and now Jon Snodgrass, Solomon Kobrin, Gilbert Geis, and Jim Short—are products not only of our backgrounds and generations but also of history. The life-course perspective thus is useful for our purposes in yet another way; that is, in evaluating the relationship of Shaw and Stanley (and others), and the work of Shaw, Henry McKay, and their collaborators, and our own interpretations. It is useful because it reminds us of the importance of history, that every cohort—and each individual—is a product of history as well as of individual variations and micro processes, and macro forces at any point in history.

Shaw touched the lives of many, including the delinquents whose life histories he collected, and those with whom he worked in treatment, colleagues at the Institute for Juvenile Research, and graduate students. His influence on each of us varied for many reasons and along many dimensions. For Stanley he became a father figure, a successful and cultured adult role model, who changed his life dramatically. While Stanley was never able to reach the level of social and economic success that Shaw represented, he attributes his turning from a life of crime and his personal ontology in no small measure to Shaw's kindness and support. Another illustration of Shaw's effect is Anthony Sorrentino, a long-time associate who grew up in Chicago's notorious Bloody Twentieth ward on the Near West Side, and became a gang worker and community organizer. Subsequently, Sorrentino worked as Shaw's administrative assistant, succeeded him as adminsitrative director of the Chicago Area Project, and later was appointed executive director of the newly formed Illinois Commission on Delinquency Prevention.[51]

Shaw opened my eyes intellectually in several ways and it was through his good offices that I secured my first full-time job in Chicago, as Secretary of the City Planning Advisory Board, while I was still a graduate student at the University of Chicago.[52] He also introduced me to Henry McKay, Sol Kobrin, Tony Sorrentino, and many others associated with the Institute for Juvenile Research and the Chicago Area Project. I continue to enjoy very much many of these associations, renewing them whenever the opportunity arises.

It was Shaw who first suggested to me that a Kinsey-type report on juvenile delinquency was needed to correct the impression created by official data that delinquency was virtually a lower-class phenomenon. I suspect Shaw (and McKay) would appreciate the mounting evidence of convergence between official data, self-reports, and victim surveys insofar as the social distribution of delinquent behavior is concerned.[53]

Shaw's ideas and the program he set in motion evidence continued vitality despite problems associated with the institutionalization of the Chicago Area Project.[54] The Area Project, and Shaw in particular, have been criticized for not systematically evaluating their efforts or allowing them to be evaluated. Criticism has been directed also at the alleged bandaid approach to problems requiring more radical change. But these, too, are matters of history. Shaw's program developed during the Great Depression, and it was radical for the time, for it championed indigenous community leadership and organization, in opposition to prevailing professional social-work and social-agency programs that were imposed from outside the local community. Comparisons, often invidious, are made between Shaw's "working within the system" approach and Alinsky's conflict approach. But Alinsky's most notable accomplishments took place during a period of intense civil-rights activity and militancy, when the Area Project already was well established and suffering some of the problems of institutionalization. The accomplishments of Alinsky's organizations have not been systematically studied, either. But there is evidence, as Bennett notes, that The Woodlawn Organization (TWO), the result of one of Alinsky's most celebrated efforts, "was most successful in what might be termed little issues that affected a relatively small number of people and could be pursued to a successful outcome with relatively meager organizational resources. A boy was kicked out of school, a woman was cheated by a merchant, a slum lord turned off the heat; These were bread-and-butter issues that helped build the organization."[55]

Sorrentino, in the second of his books, reports that the Chicago Area Project, in consultation with outside professionals, "came to the conclusion that this conflict between two theories of community organizing need no longer exist" that indeed they are complementary.[56] Recent events suggest that this may be the case at this time in history. Area Project people—individually and collectively—were successful in creating the Illinois Delinquency Prevention Commission in 1976, over the opposition of the governor and powerful elements in the state bureaucracy. They did so by mobilizing massive support in local communities and lobbying the state legislature. The effort was guided by Shaw's principles and overcame the same sorts of bureaucratic control of individuals, communities, and resources that Shaw fought against. The struggle goes on, of course, and conflicts once resolved emerge in new forms. The political victory of the Area Project people and philosophy in Illinois brought its own set of problems—bureaucratization, continued challenge by child-service agencies and professionals, and distortion of Shaw's principles by some who continue to espouse them.

The future of the Chicago Area Project, and other projects modeled after it, is by no means clear. State funding for the Delinquency Prevention Commission lapsed in July 1981 as a result it appears of political controversy and confusion. The Chicago Area Project later entered into a contract with the Department of Child and Family Services. This raises again fears of political and bureaucratic control. The Quincy Area Project has chosen, for the present at least, to raise its budget from the private sector, following Shaw's course in this respect. The old issues remain: issues of resources, control, expertise, and how to use it. For a variety of reasons, it seems likely that these issues will be joined with renewed vigor in the 1980s and beyond.

I have noted Bittner's focus on the threat of professionalization to personal autonomy and the quality of life. Cressey sounds a similar theme when he observes that basic to human rights is the problem of balancing control and personal liberty. "Are the people to be experts who make their own personal decisions? Or are they to be merely parts in a rank-oriented bureaucratic machine designed to carry out the designs of a central power, be that power a dictator or a duly elected representative assembly?"[57]

The reality of social change and the lessons of history suggest that such issues are not amenable to permanent solution. Certainly they defy solution from any simple political formula. The specific form of organized attempts to arrive at solutions doubtless will continue to be debated and, I hope, experimented with. But I suspect—and frankly, I hope—that Shaw's ideas will retain their vitality. I see no reason to abandon the appraisal I offered more than a decade ago, in writing of "the Chicago Area Project as a Social Movement:"

> Shaw was one of the first—perhaps *the* first—to see the relevance and the potential of the deeply imbedded American tradition of local autonomy and organization, self-help and self-determination, for the problems of slum dwellers. He was aware that this tradition would have to be accommodated to countervailing forces of political and economic centralization and bureaucratization, and he had the political acumen to realize that this problem could be resolved only in the course of unfolding and unforeseeable events. In the meantime, he was able to harness the mystique of the democratic ethos to enable many to begin opening doors on the corridors of power, and to open some of these doors himself, in the service of the enterprise."[58]

It seems appropriate to add, however, that the relevance of these traditions is not limited to the problems of slum dwellers. They are applicable to all segments of society. Indeed, they may prove to be fundamental to the very social fabric in a world increasingly dependent on expertise to avoid disaster in many areas of life (for example, threats associated with scientific discovery and technology) and tempted, as Bittner notes, to relinquish autonomy to experts in other areas.[59] The balance struck between reliance on experts and autonomy—whether personal, group, community, or larger aggregates of persons—will be critical to the quality of life in the future as it has been in the past. Because of the fateful nature of many of the problems with which we are confronted, it may also be critical to our very survival.

Notes

1. Howard Becker, "Introduction," in *The Jack-Roller: A Delinquent Boy's Own Story,* 2nd ed. Clifford R. Shaw (Chicago: University of Chicago Press, 1966), p. vi.

2. Clifford R. Shaw, *The Jack-Roller: A Delinquent Boy's Own Story* (Chicago: University of Chicago Press, 1930), p. 3.

3. James Bennett, *Oral History and Delinquency: The Rhetoric of Criminology* (Chicago: University of Chicago Press, 1981), pp. 193ff.

4. T.V. Smith and L.D. White, eds., *Chicago: An Experiment in Social Science* (Chicago: University of Chicago Press, 1929); Louis Wirth, ed., *Eleven Twenty-Six: A Decade of Social Science Research* (Chicago: University of Chicago Press, 1940); and James F. Short, Jr., ed., *The Social Fabric of the Metropolis: Contributions of the Chicago School of Urban Sociology* (Chicago: University of Chicago Press, 1971).

5. Robert E.L. Faris, *Chicago Sociology 1920–1932* (Chicago: University of Chicago Press, 1970), p. 88.

6. Becker, *The Jack-Roller*, p. vii.

7. Even the best recent studies of aspects of community life lack the documentation of related phenomena that characterized the work of the Chicago School. There is continuity with the early tradition in later Chicago studies: for example, Albert Hunter, *Symbolic Communities: The Persistence and Change of Chicago's Local Communities* (Chicago: University of Chicago Press, 1974); Gerald D. Suttles, *The Social Order of the Slum: Ethnicity and Territory in the Inner City* (Chicago: University of Chicago Press, 1968); and Elijah Anderson, *A Place on the Corner* (Chicago: University of Chicago Press, 1976). But we cannot supplement these studies with other types of documentation and with documentation of other phenomena that might further inform the special aspects of community life studied. This is even more true of studies in New York and Los Angeles. (For example, Francis A.J. Ianni, *Black Mafia: Ethnic Succession in Organized Crime* [New York: Simon and Schuster, 1974]; Francis A.J. Ianni and Elizabeth Reuss-Ianni, *A Family Business: Kinship and Social Control in Organized Crime* [New York: Russell Sage, 1972]; Bettylou Valentine, *Hustling and other Hard Work* [New York: Free Press, 1978]; and Joan W. Moore, Robert Garcia, Luis Carda, and Frank Valencia, *Homeboys* [Philadelphia: Temple University Press, 1978]). Much could be learned by greater utilization of further studies in these cities.

8. Bernice Naugarten, "Personality Change in Late Life: A Developmental Perspective," in *The Psychology of Adult Development and Aging,* ed. Carl Eisdorfer and M. Powell Lawton (Washington, D.C.: American Psychological Association, 1973), p. 331.

9. Shaw, *The Jack-Roller,* 1930, p. xiii. These statements were deleted from the 1966 edition.

10. Ibid., pp. 73ff.

11. Ibid., p. 162.

12. Ibid., p. 12.

13. Edwin M. Lemert, "The Juvenile Court—Quest and Realities," in *Task Force Report: Juvenile Delinquency and Youth Crime,* President's

Commission on Law Enforcement and Administration of Justice (Washington, D.C.: U.S. Government Printing Office, 1967), pp. 91-106.

14. Egon Bittner, "Autonomy and Technique: How Far May We Go Before Professional Solutions for All Problems Will Begin to Diminish Human Life?" *Society for the Study of Social Problems Newsletter,* vol. 12, no. 4 (1980):2-3.

15. Bennett, *Oral History and Delinquency,* p. 198.

16. LaMar T. Empey, *American Delinquency: Its Meaning and Construction* (Homewood, Illinois: Dorsey Press, 1968), p. 538.

17. Shaw, *The Jack-Roller,* p. 24.

18. Ibid., p. 61.

19. Solomon Kobrin, "The Chicago Area Project—A 25-year Assessment," *Annals of the American Academy of Political and Social Science* (March 1959):19-29.

20. See James F. Short, Jr., "Introduction to the Revised Edition," in *Juvenile Delinquency and Urban Areas,* Clifford R. Shaw and Henry D. McKay (Chicago: University of Chicago Press, 1969), p. xlix.

21. Bennett, *Oral History and Delinquency,* p. 198.

22. See Glen Elder, "Age Differentiation and the Life Course," in *Annual Review of Sociology,* vol. 1, ed. Alex Inkeles, James Coleman, and Neil Smelser (Palo Alto: Annual Review, 1975), pp. 165-190; and J.T. Mortimer and Roberta Simmons, "Adult Socialization," in *Annual Review of Sociology,* vol. 4, ed. Ralph H. Turner, James Coleman, and Renee C. Fox (Palo Alto: Annual Reviews, 1978), pp. 421-454.

23. Shaw, *The Jack-Roller,* p. 47.

24. Ibid., pp. 190-191.

25. Shaw, *The Jack-Roller,* p. 197.

26. The Jack-Roller et al., *The Jack-Roller at Seventy,* ch. 11.

27. Ibid.

28. O.G. Brim, Jr., "Socialization through the Life Cycle," in Socialization After Childhood, ed. O.G. Brim, Jr. and Stanton Wheeler (New York: Wiley, 1966), pp. 1-49.

29. Eugene A. Weinstein, "The Development of Interpersonal Competence," in *Handbook of Socialization Theory and Research,* ed. David A. Goslin (Chicago: Rand McNally, 1969), p. 753.

30. James F. Short, Jr. and Fred L. Strodtbeck, *Group Process and Gang Delinquency* (Chicago: University of Chicago Press, 1974) p. 236.

31. Compare Shaw, *The Jack-Roller,* pp. 198-199; and Short and Strodtbeck, *Group Process and Gang Delinquency,* p. 238.

32. Short and Strodtbeck, *Group Process and Gang Delinquency,* p. 236.

33. Weinstein, *Handbook,* p. 769.

34. Agnes Hankiss, "Ontologies of the Self: On the Mythological Rearranging of One's Life-history," in *Biography and Society: The Life History*

Approach in the Social Sciences, ed. Daniel Bertaux (Beverly Hills: Sage *Publications,* 1981), p. 203.

35. Marjorie Fishe Lowenthal and David Chiriboga, "Social Stress and Adaptation: toward a Life-course Perspective," in *The Psychology of Adult Development and Aging,* ed. Carl Eisdorfer and M. Powell Lawton (Washington, D.C.: American Psychological Association, 1973), p. 289.

36. Shaw, *The Jack-Roller,* p. 47.

37. Lowenthal and Chiriboga, *Psychology of Adult Development and Aging,* p. 287.

38. Ibid., p. 289.

39. Marjorie Fishe Lowenthal, Majda Thurner, David Chiriboga, and associates, *Four Stages of Life* (San Francisco: Jossey-Bass, 1975), p. 233.

40. Ibid., p. 225.

41. Ibid., p. 230.

42. John Clausen, "Foreword," in *Children of the Great Depression,* Glen Elder (Chicago: University of Chicago Press, 1974), pp. xvii-xviii; see also Matilda Riley, Marilyn Johnson, and Anne Foner, *Aging and Society: A Sociology of Age Stratification* (New York: Russell Sage Foundation, 1972).

43. S. Thernstrom, *The Other Bostonians: Poverty and Progress in the American Metropolis, 1880-1970* (Cambridge, Massachusetts: Harvard University Press, 1973).

44. Elder, *Annual Review of Sociology,* p. 185.

45. See, for example, Ruben Hill, *Family Development in Three Generations* (Cambridge, Massachusetts: Schenkman, 1970); Elder, *Children of the Great Depression;* and Lowenthal et al., *Four Stages of Life.*

46. Lowenthal et al., *Four Stages of Life,* p. 237.

47. Ibid., p. 145.

48. Jon Snodgrass, "The American Criminological Tradition: Portraits of the Men and Ideology in a Discipline," (Ph.D. diss. University of Pennsylvania, 1972).

49. Shaw, *The Jack-Roller,* pp. 194-195.

50. Bennett, *Oral History and Delinquency,* p. 197.

51. See Anthony Sorrentino, *Organizing Against Crime: Redeveloping the Neighborhood* (New York: Human Sciences Press, 1977). Sorrentino's life course appears similar to that of William Foote Whyte's research assistant, Angelo Ralph Orlandella (Sam Franco) in the type of influence exerted on him by his mentor (see William Foote Whyte, *Street Corner Society: The Social Structure of an Italian Slum,* 2nd ed. Chicago: University of Chicago Press, 1981). In both cases the men learned conventional skills that later proved to be valuable in their careers. Shaw's influence on Stanley apparently was not of this type but rather was directed toward the treatment program devised by Shaw. It is frequently the case that those who are the object of treatment programs—detached worker pro-

grams with gangs, for example—are attracted to careers like the careers of those treating them.

52. I have discussed this appointment and other aspects of my personal and professional career in Irving Louis Horowitz, "The Natural History of One Sociological Career," in *Sociological Self-Images: A Collective Portrait* (Beverly Hills: Sage Publications, 1969), pp. 117-132. Choice of the title for this chapter also was influenced by Shaw.

53. See M. Hindelang, Travis Hirschi, and Joseph Weis, *Measuring Delinquency* (Beverly Hills: Sage Publications, 1981); Delbert S. Elliott, Brian A. Knowles, and Rachelle J. Canter, *The Epidemiology of Delinquent Behavior and Drug Use Among American Adolescents* (Boulder, Colorado: Behavioral Research Institute, 1981).

54. See Harold Finestone, *Victims of Change: Juvenile Delinquents in America* (Chicago: University of Chicago Press, 1976); Bennett, *Oral History and Delinquency.*

55. Bennett, *Oral History and Delinquency,* p. 217, quoting John Hall Fish, *Black Power/White Control* (Princeton: Princeton University Press, 1973).

56. Anthony Sorrentino, *How to Organize the Neighborhood for Delinquency Prevention* (New York: Human Sciences Press, 1979), p. 11.

57. Donald R. Cressey, "Crime, Science, and Bureaucratic Rules," *The Center Magazine* (July/August 1978):40-48.

58. Short, *Juvenile Delinquency and Urban Areas,* p. xlix.

59. Egon Bittner, "Autonomy and Technique."

References

Bertaux, Daniel, ed. 1981. *Biography and Society: The Life History Approach in the Social Sciences.* Beverly Hills: Sage Publications.

Goslin, David, ed. 1969. *Handbook of Socialization: Theory and Research.* Chicago: Rand McNally.

Hughes, Helen MacGill. 1961. *The Fantastic Lodge: The Autobiography of a Girl Drug Addict.* Cambridge, Massachusetts: Houghton Mifflin.

Hunter, Albert. 1974. *Symbolic Communities: The Persistence and Change of Chicago's Local Communities.* Chicago: University of Chicago Press.

Rice, Stuart A. 1931. "Hypotheses and verifications in Clifford R. Shaw's studies of juvenile delinquency." In *Methods in Social Science: A Case Book.* Stuart A. Rice, ed. Chicago: University of Chicago Press. pp. 549-565.

25 The Uses of the Life-History Document for the Development of Delinquency Theory

Solomon Kobrin

The publication of Stanley's "own story" of his adult years offers an occasion for focusing once again on the issues and controversies that followed Shaw's publication in 1930 of *The Jack-Roller*.[1] The appearance of that book, describing in Stanley's own words his delinquency career during his childhood and youth, raised the question of the value and place of the case study in sociological analysis. It appeared during a period when there was still active concern with the development of sociology as a generalizing science. The case study, then as now, was employed commonly by clinicians in the analysis of problem behavior in the individual for purposes of treatment intervention.

The question of the value for systematic knowledge of crime and delinquency of a case study in the form of a life-history document was initially answered in a number of ways. It was seen as furnishing background information for the development of testable hypotheses.[2] Another justification was its use in explicating the concept of *social type* as distinguished from personality pattern in the understanding of role behavior.[3] Shaw himself offered a modest response to his critics. He was sharply aware of the limited value of the case study in developing general propositions for a theory of delinquency. But in rejoinder to those who questioned its value "for purposes of scentific generalization because of its subjective and non-quantitative character," he replied: "[N]evertheless it seems to be true that there are many aspects of delinquency which are not susceptible to treatment by formal statistical methods."[4]

With the reissue of *The Jack-Roller* thirty-six years later, Becker, who provided an introduction, suggested additional uses of the life-history document.[5] Among others, it can serve as a test of the adequacy of theory purporting to explain delinquency, provide insight into the subjective side of institutional processes, and suggest neglected variables in theory building. These are typically the more elusive elements of deviant behavior that are often difficult to capture in quantifiable variables and represent the neglected aspects of the problem that Shaw attempted to describe in his use of life-history documents.

Shaw's devotion to this method may be understood in the light of the intellectual tradition and background of theory and observation that framed his perspective and interests. These were derived from the Chicago School of Sociology as developed during the 1920s in the work of Robert E. Park, W.I. Thomas, George Herbert Mead, and Ernest W. Burgess. The key to this tradition was the idea of diversity as the central feature of an urban society unified primarily at the symbiotic level.[6] Park and his students viewed society as a mosaic of groups, each inhabiting marginally divergent moral worlds, representing a variant adaptation of a common stock of culture symbols, and tending to ascribe variant meaning to these symbols. The view of diversity at the group level had its counterpart at the level of individual behavior in an emphasis on the diversity of meanings that nominally similar events and experiences might have for different persons. This notion was expressed by W.I. Thomas in the observation that crucial to the understanding of an item of behavior in response to any situation was the manner in which the person defined the meaning that the situation had for him.[7]

The full development of this approach to the analysis of human social behavior was accomplished by Mead through his theory of *symbolic interaction* in the genesis of the social act.[8] He, too, while adducing the general principles underlying the emergence of a "self" as the crucial orienting object in human social behavior, the empirical focus was on the concrete acts of significant others. These function not as simple stimuli: the response is instead mediated by an act of interpretation and evaluation; in brief, by a "definition of the situation" as it arises in the context of interpersonal relationships.

It should be noted in this connection that the importance of taking account of the subjectivity of human social behavior has long been recognized in the work of sociologists. The problem first became the center of spirited controversy among German sociologists of the late nineteenth century and was ultimately clarified by Weber.[9] It concerned the question of the distinctiveness of the social in contrast to the "natural" sciences. Weber defined the distinctiveness of the social sciences as consisting in the importance of the meaning that actors attach to their social acts. Although enunciated early in the development of modern sociology, this methodological principle has been largely ignored in the behavioral objectivism that has characterized most contemporary sociology. Its implementation became the concern almost exclusively of a specialized branch of sociology pursued by Mead's followers and devoted to the exploration of the sources and dynamics of meaning and intention as these enter as determinants in human social action. In contrast to a prevailing implicit imagery of man as responding directly to the external pressures of social forces, whether of culture or structure, the image these writers have promulgated is of man as a processor of these influences, with a capacity to judge their significance for him in the concrete situations he confronts, define their meanings, and choose a course of action in response.

Despite their general neglect, these ideas have entered the body of socio-logical thought in a variety of forms: in Weber's attention to subjective meaning as grounds for the conduct of the social actor,[10] in Parsons's *voluntarism*,[11] in the phenomenology of Schutz,[12] and of Berger and Luckmann,[13] and in the concept of *reflexivity*.[14] And it was precisely this component of subjectivity, of the actor's perception and interpretation of the meaning of his experience, that Shaw had reference to in speaking of the aspect of delin-quent behavior that "eluded quantitative studies." In his view, it was this element in its patterned form over time that had to be taken into account in a theory of delinquency.

A clear implication of this view is the requirement that a theory of crime and delinquency include a social-psychological component within a frame-work of structural determinants. This appears to be lacking, at least in sys-tematically developed form, in the three currently prominent theories of delinquency: strain, labeling, and the social-control theory recently devel-oped by Hirschi.[15] This integration was absent as well in the cultural-transmission theory, an earlier influential theory for which, paradoxically, Shaw was largely responsible.

For example, in *cultural-transmission theory*, the central proposition holds that in the social conditions found in the delinquency areas the norms of a delinquent subculture were learned just as are any other items of culture. However, the notion that the learning process may be treated as a constant instead of a variable is questionable. In strain theory the condi-tions are unclear under which the tension between the culturally ordained goals and limitation of the means to achieve them results in deviant be-havior.[16] Nor can we be certain when and for whom being labeled as a de-viant by official fiat induces an acceptance of the label by the person. Although current social-control theory has a social-psychological orienta-tion, it is not explicit regarding the specific content of interpersonal rela-tions in which the controls associated with attachment to conventional authorities and commitment to their norms and values are invariably proof against persistent deviance.[17]

In brief, there is not yet in hand a general theory that embraces the struc-tural as well as the social-psychological factors implicated in crime and delin-quency. Only with such theory can we begin to understand why substantial numbers of lower class, male, minority group youth do not become per-sistently delinquent, and why somewhat reduced numbers of male youth in the structurally favored populations do. In the absence of tested theory of this type, we shall remain with theories of limited predictive utility, restricted in their refinements to small increases in the statistician's *explained variance* that still leave in the dark large areas of deviant phenomena.

Having considered these issues, we may now return to the question of the possible uses of the life-history document. The caution must of course be raised that a single case has little value for purposes of generalization. So far, however, as it may provide a negative instance confuting or throwing into question the claims of established theories, the single case can suggest how they may be usefully improved. No general theory can escape the challenge of the negative instance; that is, the case in a series that it does not account for. But negative cases also represent a critical resource for the task of recasting general theory to increase its predictive power. While systematic use of negative cases has been suggested for this purpose through use of the method of *analytic induction,*[18] or of *grounded theory,*[19] it has not been taken up by criminologists. It remains, therefore, that the single life-history document affords no more than a passing opportunity to comment on the extent to which the facts of the case are explained by current theories.

It is also necessary to note that the life history of the type presented in this book is a selective version of the totality of the person's life experience. However, no such account can be otherwise. In the standard autobiography, the person similarly engages in an exercise of retrospective reconstruction in which incidents and experiences are selected out of the recalled flow of events to create an instructive, self-congratulatory, or tragic picture of his life. On the other hand, the life history of the type included in this book has the considerable merit of a product created by an interviewer whose prompting questions are guided by an interest in the understanding of deviant behavior. A concern, for example, with the understanding of political or economic behavior, of course, could elicit a life-history document of quite different emphasis and content. The persona of the individual that emerges from any life-history document is literally created by himself or others.

These injunctions notwithstanding, Stanley's account of his adult years offers an opportunity to examine the fit of the theories mentioned to the facts of the jack-roller's later life. It is clear that Stanley's is a case of an incorrigible delinquent who reformed. His reformation is attested to, very simply, by the fact whatever other forms of unconventional activity he engaged in, it did not include either serious or persistent law violation. We turn to the examination of cultural transmission, strain, labeling, and social-control theory in relation to the facts of Stanley's reformation. So far as these theories purport to explain the genesis of criminal careers they should serve also to account for their termination.

Cultural-Transmission Theory

As exemplified in the work of Shaw and Shaw and McKay,[20] cultural-transmission theory includes one form of social-control theory as well as what was later termed *differential-association theory.*[21] There is a little question that the biographical materials of *The Jack-Roller* fully reflect the operation early in the life of Stanley of processes of weakened family and neighborhood control of the conduct of the young, of opportunity to learn the prevailing pattern of delinquency endemic in the ecological setting of neighborhoods of the type described, and of progressive association exclusively with other active delinquents. Moreover, in offering a sanguine view of Stanley's reformation at the end of five years of treatment, Shaw attributed the outcome to the new and now conventional settings of home and work to which he had succeeded in introducing Stanley. Indeed, in this book Stanley acknowledges with gratitude the importance of the changed social environment in inducing him to abandon a life of crime.

However, if we exclude forms of deviance other than crime, the same set of explanatory principles cannot account for the durability of Stanley's reformation. A theory of cultural determinism, with its social control and differential association components, would lead one to expect that his adult life was marked by stable and consistent association with conventional others whose anticrime values and prosocial expectations had been incorporated as internalized controls. On the contrary, his adult experience was in fact one of continuous disruption and instability in the intimate sphere of marriage and family life as well as in the long succession of jobs he held. Moreover, while he no longer retained contact with the offenders he had known earlier, neither did he attempt nor could he confine his associations to persons drawn from the respectable strata of society.

While he found warm friendships with conventional others, the disruptions and instability of his adult life left him socially most comfortable with what can only be considered marginally deviant types. Among these were persons who shared his occasional addiction to gambling, the residents of a house of prostitution in one reported episode, an exmental patient with whom he had shared a common experience of incarceration in a mental hospital, and, late in his life, homeless and alcoholic habituees of a public park. The point is that in a long crime-free adult life following on an early career as an incorrigible delinquent, there is little to suggest that the reformation was a product of the consistent embrace of prosocial cultural influences.

Strain Theory

Cultural-transmission theory took as a given the existence in the delinquency areas of a delinquent subculture. Apart from accounting for the geographic location of delinquency areas as an effect of urban ecological processes, it did not treat the emergence and persistence of the subculture as problematic. This issue, in turn, formed the research agenda of such subsequent theorists as Cohen, Merton, and Cloward and Ohlin.[22] Although

there were differences in the way they accounted for the origin of the delinquent subculture, their theories all focused on the location of lower-class
youth in the social-class structure of urban society. For each, that location
was productive of *strain*; that is, of some form of subjective discomfort arising from discrepant pressures and expectations to which delinquent behavior
was seen as a necessary adaptation. For Cohen, the strain stemmed from a
sense of devalued status resulting from the trained inability of lower-class
boys to conform to the behavioral and achievement expectations of the
middle-class authorities in control of educational and other socializing institutions. Merton, on the other hand, viewed the strain as a consequence of
the discrepancy between the acceptance by lower-class boys of the general
culture values of monetary success and lack of opportunity to achieve the
goal through conventional means. Cloward and Ohlin elaborated Merton's
means-ends schema by accounting for variant patterns of delinquency that
resulted from patterned variation in the types of nonconventional and il-
legitimate opportunities for personal, social, or monetary success differen-
tially available to a population of lower-class boys.

How does Stanley's account of his adult career square with the
structural-functional tenets of strain theory? Neither the Cohen nor the
Cloward and Ohlin versions of the theory purport to explain delinquency in
the individual case; its aim is to explain only the emergence and persistence
of their postulated delinquent subculture. Cohen in particular points out
that delinquent behavior in any individual may arise quite simply from his
exposure to the existing delinquent practices of street peer groups in which
he seeks acceptance. We do not know whether Stanley's early delinquencies
were a response to such exposure, or whether during his youth he con-
sciously experienced either status or opportunity frustration. However, in
his current biography he does report a very real concern with the problem of
denigrated status as an adult. A theme that emerges with some prominence
is his aspiration to "make it" financially, his continual striving to achieve at
the least a stable and secure income, and at the same time his consistent
failure to succeed in this effort. Add to this the skills he had learned in com-
mitting offenses and his later acquisition of some of the skills of the confidence man in the course of his work as a salesman, as well as access, if he
wished, to currently active offenders. These represent all the elements of the
blocked opportunity version of strain theory. Had Stanley continued into a
career of adult crime, they could well have been regarded as explaining this
outcome. As to the matter of status frustration, which he felt sharply, this
seems to have developed only after he had acquired new and now middle-
class reference groups which, if anything, should have exacerbated his
status problem and provided a strong impetus for a return to crime. Neither
blocked opportunity nor status frustration proved the undoing of his reformation.

Labeling Theory

Briefly, the claim of the labeling theorists is that the formal processing of deviants by social-control agents operates as a significant factor in the formation of the person's self-concept as a deviant.[23] In turn, the deviant self-concept then becomes the basis for the restriction of the person's membership to supportive groups of similar types of deviants. Through such group association the deviant behavior becomes fixed as an attribute of the person.

Little in Stanley's account of his juvenile experience presented in *The Jack-Roller* is illuminated by labeling theory. If we take the main tenet of the theory to mean that the person who is formally processed as a deviant by agents of social control is constrained to accept this definition as a self-concept, the evidence in Stanley's case is quite the contrary. He viewed his repeated experiences of incarceration during his juvenile years as a painful sojourn in enemy country, posing simply a problem of survival with least pain. However, evidence in his adult biography suggest that the labeling process operated in a somewhat complex way. If his experience as a juvenile left behind a residue in the form of a delinquent self-concept, it was not until he encountered the changed primary groups in his living and working situations into which Shaw introduced him. It was only at that point that he was enabled to view his earlier self from the perspective of conventional and law-abiding primary groups. Suggested in these passages of his adult biography is that the person's self-concept emerges as a meaningful element in the control of behavior only at moments of change in primary group membership.

In this connection, Finestone's emendation of labeling theory permits its application in Stanley's case.[24] He points out that the labeling consequences of processing by agents of formal control occurs only when their definition of the person is taken over by significant others in his primary groups. Only when use is made of the resources of reward and punishment, of approval and disapproval, through which the processes of spontaneous social control operate, is it likely that self-definition as a deviant will result. We can say that Stanley acquired post hoc a self-concept as a delinquent as a consequence of formal processing, but only at a later point when he took over the perspective of primary groups for whom the label "delinquent" was a meaningful social judgment. Having now defined his youthful self as delinquent, Stanley faced the labeling and self-concept issue as a lifelong concern in the effort to sustain his reformation. In this light, we may appreciate the self-disparagement in his rendering as comedy the attempted robbery-with-gun, the single instance of serious backsliding. Similarly, passages describing his efforts to maintain a conventional marriage and family life reveal an awareness of their value as validating his claim to respectability. Here again the caution should be raised that we may be dealing with another instance of reconstructive reinterpretation of past events as seen from Stanley's seventy-year-old vantage point. But no matter: the fact is that in any event self-concept as an effect of labeling processes is invariably a product of the reconstruction of the meaning of past events. The point is that the perspective from which past events are interpreted is that which reflect the sense of the person of his current significant primary group memberships.

Social-Control Theory

There remains, finally, currently influential social-control theory as presented by Hirschi.[25] Unlike its place in the cultural determinism of Shaw and McKay, in which behavioral control is viewed as a direct effect of learned group norms, Hirschi's conception of the social-control process centers on a number of *social-psychological variables.* The variables are defined as those which "bond" the person to the prevailing moral values of the wider society. Whether the person becomes a delinquent and continues to engage in delinquent activity, he contends, will depend on the strength of his attachment to and identification with such conventional adult authorities as parents and teachers, commitment to their values, belief in the validity and legitimacy of those values, and involvement in activities expressive of these orientations. The probability of a delinquent and, by extension, of an adult criminal career is a function of the strength of these variables.

Although it was developed to account for the genesis of delinquent careers, the theory should in principle be capable of explaining the termination of a delinquent career, such as occurred in Stanley's case. Hirsch's control theory has the virtue of accounting simultaneously and substantively for conformity and deviance within the same parsimonious set of propositions. As a case of reformation, at least so far as criminal activity was concerned, Stanley became a conformist. The question thus becomes: How well do the factors of attachment, commitment, involvement, and belief explain the reversal of his earlier well-established pattern of criminal activity?

There is no reason not to take at face value Stanley's warm, not to say extravagant, acknowledgment of Shaw's role in turning him away from criminal pursuits. As is typical of those endowed with native therapeutic skills, of which they are generally unaware, Shaw was inclined to credit signs of reformation in Stanley to the use of theoretically based treatment procedures.'' His present behavior trends, interests, and philosophy of life,'' he states at the end of a five-year treatment program, ''have developed as a product of his participation in the life of conventional social groups.''[26] However this may be, on the basis of Stanley's appraisal of

Shaw's significance in his life, there can be little question that a deep personal attachment was formed. Similarly, there is evidence of attachment to the members of the family with whom Stanley found a first home after release from his last imprisonment. In short, the criterion of Hirschi's attachment to conventional others is clearly met.

However, the evidence is more tenuous respecting the additional three factors postulated by the theory as essential in bonding the persons to a pattern of conformity. Indeed, as we move from attachment to commitment to involvement to belief, the evidence for their operation progressively weakens. As an aspect of his newly established attachments, Stanley's commitment to lawful conduct remains robust, with only a single and unrepeated lapse. But there appears to have been no consistent involvement in conventional activities throughout the long span of his adult years. His work history primarily as a salesman reveals a basic instability due in part to the nature of the occupation and in part to his egocentric truculence. Moreover, his preferred recreational activities were characteristically only marginally conventional. As noted earlier, he was socially most comfortable in the company of deviant social types. He also confesses that he found extremely irksome the constraints and responsibilities of marriage and domesticity, possibly a result in part of a troublesome not to say disastrous first marriage. Thus neither his occupational career nor his recreational pattern reflect a durable and consistent involvement in conventional activity.

As to the element of belief in the validity of the standard moral norm, there is little in Stanley's adult biography to indicate the salience of the question for him. It is likely in any case that this is the kind of question that becomes problematic principally for philosophers of ethics and for respondents to questionnaires. For the latter, reflection on this issue is an unaccustomed exercise that generally elicits the received opinion of the community. Stanley's view of the validity of conventional moral values can be inferred only from the report he has provided of the action choices he made in situations presenting a moral dilemma. And even there, it is not possible to judge whether the choice made was based on pragmatic or value considerations. Among others, one such episode is illustrative.

When his suspicions were confirmed that his wife's refusal to help him obtain a discharge from the mental hospital was motivated by her reputed extramarital affair, he confronted her in a homicidal rage. The situation presented many of the features of domestic conflicts that sometimes result in homicide and frequently in aggravated assault—the suffering he had endured in what he regarded as an unjust and humiliating incarceration in a mental hospital, the insult to his manhood in having been cuckolded, and his explosive temper that had repeatedly led him into assaultive violence. Yet, in the face of provocation, justification, and a capacity for violence, Stanley controlled his rage and walked away from the encounter.

It is not likely that this choice of action came from an acquired moral repugnance for violence as there were later episodes in which he was assaultive. Or, as seems more likely, after a long period of separation from his wife and the decline of the meaning of his earlier attachment to her, had the sting of personal insult subsided sufficiently to undo whatever gratification there might have been in physical assault? And, as still another possibility, did he find sufficient moral and symbolic retaliatory gratification in the simple fact of confronting his wife with proofs of her guilt? All of these possibilities, and others, point up the complexity of the elements that can enter into the ways in which the person may construe the meaning for himself of a situation of interpersonal conflict. Of these, only one may be a belief in some principle of conduct, whose scope and determinacy is likely to be limited in ways virtually impossible to ascertain as it competes with a host of other urgent interests.

Where Stanley does feel called on to state his beliefs, they have been limited to expressions of patriotic sentiment and the endorsement of a code of loyalty and fairness in interpersonal relations. He also extols the virtues of a life of labor devoted to winning security and a modicum of affluence, although never in all his years was he able to muster the discipline and self-control to achieve this. And nowhere does he exhibit a belief in the conventional norms condemning vice activities. On balance, the element of belief appears to be present, but hardly as more than a weak variable.

How well, then, does Hirschi's social-psychological control theory account for the substantial reformation Stanley underwent in the course of his adult life? There is evidence that both attachment and commitment were prominent in this development. However, commitment to a law-abiding life showed much weaker relationship to involvement in activities, both occupational and recreational, capable of implementing the commitment, with the important exception of his embrace of marriage and domesticity. And while the theory postulates a strong and direct relationship between attachment and belief,[27] it would hardly be true that Stanley adopted the moral code by which Shaw lived, despite the profound respect in which he held him.

But because a theory does not precisely fit the fact of an individual case does not mean it is in error. It means instead that it has hold of only part of the explanation of the phenomenon of interest. The social-psychological variables employed in the type of social-control theory considered here would be unlikely, unless extensively qualified, to account for a very large proportion of cases of either conformity or deviance. As developed in Hirschi's work, its shortcoming seems to be its exclusion of the problem of motivation as a critical variable in behavior. The argument justifying the exclusion of motivation is that the types of motives adduced by some criminologists to account for delinquent behavior, such as a drive for winning status in a delinquent peer group, a desire for material goods, a need to ex-

hibit courage and male hubris, or a wish to enjoy forbidden adult gratifica-
tions, account equally for many forms of lawful behavior.[28] Such motivational theories, therefore, do not distinguish delinquent from nondelinquent
behavior.

However, motivation so conceived has been confounded with generalized
interests. Motivation reasonably may be distinguished from the latter as the
pursuit of such interest within some structure of constraints originating,
remotely or proximately, in the social and physical resources available to
persons at various social locations and in the personal resources that can be
mobilized in interpersonal relationships. If it means anything, social control
refers precisely to these constraints, internalized in the specific sense that,
being habitually taken into account, they enter into the construction of
social acts as morally valid. Thus, one may, as a semantic convenience,
regard any of the general interests alluded to as a specific motivation but
recognize that any one of them can have quite different behavioral out-
comes under the conditions affecting the operation of the social-control
process. It is, then, not interest as motivation that differentiates delinquents
from nondelinquents, but the behavioral shape the expression of the interest
assumes under the specific conditions of constraint that variously result in
deviance or conformity.

In brief, the concepts of attachment, commitment, involvement, and
belief are useful as labels that describe, after the fact, processes and events
that have been at play in producing either deviants or conformists. There is
indeed a gain in conceptual clarity, but again only at the descriptive level,
for a proposition of the following type: The failure of the person to become
emotionally attached to conventional norm givers, develop a commitment
to and a belief in the moral validity of those norms, and spend time in activities consonant with and expressive of those norms will result in non-
conforming or deviant behavior of some kind.

For purposes of explanation and prediction, however, we will want
some specification of the conditions under which the failure, and therefore
the deviance, occurs. In one sense, much of the corpus of delinquency
research has been concerned with such specifications. They have variously
suggested a variety of such conditions, familiar to students of delinquency
and other forms of deviance. The point is that even the conditions associated with, for example, social class, ethnicity, age, gender, and similar
descriptors of social location are themselves variables as, at the level of
behavior, their meanings are taken into account by the actor in his development of a stable pattern of action. The problem thus becomes that of dis-
cerning the regularities in the ways persons of defined categories perceive
the meanings they attribute to elements of social location. It is in this sense
that a theory of social control and deviance cannot be fully developed without incorporating into it the social-psychological processes that link the

factors of social structure at both the macro and the small group levels to the forms of concrete behavior of classes of persons.

The place of the life-history document, such as Stanley has provided, is as a primary empirical source of suggestion for leads in uncovering just these processes. In its development as a science, sociology has ignored at its peril its ultimate *explanandum* the behavior of the human being. In his presidential address in 1964 to the American Sociological Association titled "Bringing Men Back In," George Homans lectured his fellow sociologists on this point. While his vision of human behavior as the product of the balance men calculate between rewards and punishments may be faulted, his plea deserves attention. The publication in this book of the sequel to *The Jack-Roller* has brought in one man and his account of how it happened that he did not remain an incorrigible delinquent.

Notes

1. Clifford R. Shaw, *The Jack-Roller: A Delinquent Boy's Own Story* (Chicago: University of Chicago Press, 1930).

2. Stuart A. Rice, "Hypotheses and Verifications in Clifford R. Shaw's Studies of Juvenile Delinquency," in *Methods in Social Science: A Case Book*, ed. Stuart A. Rice (Chicago: University of Chicago Press, 1931).

3. Ernest W. Burgess, "Discussion," in *The Jack-Roller: A Delinquent Boy's Own Story*, Clifford R. Shaw (Chicago: University of Chicago Press, 1930), p. 185.

4. Shaw, *The Jack-Roller*, p. 21.

5. Howard S. Becker, "Introduction," in *The Jack-Roller: A Delinquent Boy's Own Story*, Clifford R. Shaw (Chicago: University of Chicago Press, 1966).

6. Robert E. Park, *On Social Control and Collective Behavior* (Chicago: University of Chicago Press, 1967).

7. W.I. Thomas and Dorothy Swaine Thomas, *The Child in America* (New York: Alfred A. Knopf, 1928).

8. George H. Mead, *Mind, Self, and Society* (Chicago: University of Chicago Press, 1934).

9. Talcott Parsons, *The Structure of Social Action*, vol. 2 (New York: The Free Press), pp. 579-586.

10. Max Weber, *The Theory of Social and Economic Organization*, trans. Talcott Parsons and A.M. Henderson (Glencoe, Illinois: The Free Press, 1947), pp. 98-99.

11. Talcott Parsons, *The Structure of Social Action*, vol. I (New York: The Free Press, 1949), p. 396.

12. Alfred Schutz, *Collected Papers*, ed. Maurice Natanson (The Hague: Nijhoff, 1962).

13. Peter Berger and Thomas Luckmann, *The Social Construction of Reality* (Garden City, New York: Doubleday, 1966).

14. Alvin W. Gouldner, *The Coming Crisis of Western Sociology* (New York: Basic Books, 1970).

15. Travis Hirschi, *Causes of Delinquency* (Berkeley: University of California Press, 1969).

16. Edwin M. Lemert, *Human Deviance, Social Problems, and Social Control* (Englewood Cliffs, New Jersey: Prentice-Hall, 1967), pp. 3-30.

17. Hirschi, *Causes of Delinquency*, pp. 16-26.

18. Alfred R. Lindesmith, *Opiate Addiction* (Bloomington, Indiana: Principia Press, 1947).

19. Barney G. Glaser and Anselm L. Strauss, *The Discovery of Grounded Theory: Strategies for Qualitative Research* (Chicago: Aldine Publishing Co., 1967).

20. Shaw, *The Jack Roller*; Clifford R. Shaw and Henry D. McKay, *Social Factors in Juvenile Delinquency: Report on the Causes of Crime*, vol. 2 (Washington, D.C.: National Commission on Law Observance and Enforcement, 1931); Clifford R. Shaw and Henry D. McKay, *Juvenile Delinquency and Urban Areas* (Chicago: University of Chicago Press, 1942).

21. Edwin H. Sutherland and Donald R. Cressey, *Criminology* (New York: Lippincott, 1974), pp. 74-91.

22. Albert K. Cohen, *Delinquent Boys: The Culture of the Gang* (New York: The Free Press, 1955); Robert K. Merton, *Social Theory and Social Structure* (New York: The Free Press, 1957); and Richard A. Cloward and Lloyd E. Ohlin, *Delinquency and Opportunity: A Theory of Delinquent Gangs* (New York: The Free Press, 1960).

23. Howard S. Becker, *Outsiders: Studies in the Sociology of Deviance* (New York: The Free Press, 1967); and Edwin M. Schur, *Labeling Deviant Behavior* (New York: Harper and Row, 1971).

24. Harold Finestone, *Victims of Change: Juvenile Delinquents in American Society* (Westport, Connecticut: Greenwood Press, 1976), pp. 211-215.

25. Hirschi, *Causes of Delinquency*.

26. Shaw, *The Jack-Roller*, 2nd ed., p. 183.

27. Hirschi, *Causes of Delinquency*, pp. 29-30.

28. Ibid., pp. 31-34.

Reference

Shaw, Clifford R. 1929. *Delinquency Areas*. Chicago: University of Chicago Press.

26 A Note on Stanley's Psychology

Jon Snodgrass

I would like to begin my brief discussion of Stanley's case by drawing attention to a repetitive pattern in his behavior. By *pattern* I mean that there is a structure or form to his actions that appears time after time. The phenomenon is evident throughout the autobiographies and interviews, but I am unable to give it an exact name. I would like to describe the pattern as expressed by the Jack-Roller in several illustrations. By relying on the text we can identify and examine the pattern in Stanley's "own vocabulary."

Just as earliest memories may reveal something characteristic about an individual, one of Stanley's comments in the first story about himself at the youngest age contains the nucleus of the theme recurrent in his conduct: "All in all, I was a rather conceited little boy who thought himself superior to the other boys of his age; and I didn't miss impressing that little thing upon their minds."[1] This recollection from the time he was about five years old indicates that Stanley acted on his need to impress his superiority on other little boys. It is the behavioral expression of this emotional need that is patterned in Stanley's life.

As a second example, if we look to Stanley's delinquencies, the central issue in the original volume, there is a description of first getting into trouble in the company of bigger boys, particularly an older stepbrother William, and a friend, Tony. "To my child-seeing eyes, I visioned Tony as a great leader in the neighborhood, and he directed his gang around with much bravado. He and William were always stealing and talking about stealing and I fell in with them as soon as I began to play around in the neighborhood."[2] In the text Stanley seems to say that he carried out the delinquent expectations of the older boys to impress them and acquire their companionship. The need for attention and admiration by others he considers superior, in order to feel superior himself, is presented as his motive for the early delinquencies. Stanley was subsequently to learn that he was unable to commit a crime on his own. "One day my partner didn't show up, and right then and there I lost all my nerve. I needed someone with me to steal. I was too cowardly to steal alone. A companion made me brave and gave me a sense of security. I couldn't to save my soul steal a dime alone."[3]

If we follow Stanley's account of how his delinquent career developed, he explains that he learned in institutions from more experienced boys to whom he looked for approval. This process is clear in the Detention Home when he was six years old:

Well do I remember how Pat Maloney impressed my childish mind. He was seven years my senior, a big, husky Irish lad, and a "master bandit." He was in for stealing automobiles, burglary, and "bumming" from home and school. . . . The young guys, me included, looked up to him. He paraded among us like a king on dress parade. My feelings of pride swelled to the breaking point when he picked me out and took a liking to me. He must have pitied me, for I was little and frail and timid.[4]

Stanley seems to want to compensate for feeling "little and frail and timid" by acting like someone he considers to be exactly the opposite. He behaves as if he wants others who are big and strong to respect him so that he can feel big and strong himself. The effort to possess others' good will toward him, by doing exactly what he imagines they want of him, appears like a leitmotif in Stanley's life history.

The feelings of importance that he attempts to acquire from others, he apparently is unable to provide for himself. This indicates that he may feel inwardly the reverse of the way he acts outwardly. In structural terms, acting superior is the manifest, or behavioral side, of the latent, or emotional side, of feeling inferior. The pattern is that behavior and emotion are related inversely in Stanley's case: Stanely acts superior to avoid feeling inferior.

The above pattern can also be sketched in Stanley's relationship with Shaw and is evident particularly in the material concerning the first year of treatment. For instance, Stanley describes an emotional transformation as a result of his initial contact:

I arrived at my destination and started to ring the bell, but hesitated because of fear of meeting anyone in my rags. Driven by necessity, I rang the bell and was admitted. Mr. Shaw greeted me warmly and pleasantly. I started to apologize for coming and for coming in my rags, but he interrupted by saying, "Forget it, sit down and make yourself comfortable." He was very happy that I had come, and said that he would get a job and a new home for me. He already had a new set of clothes for me, which I put on immediately. That made me feel much more respectable. Mr. Shaw's friend came in, and we all sat around talking that entire afternoon. I got to telling about my experiences, and they showed great interest, and the day passed before I knew it. We all went out to dinner and spent the evening together. I got a great kick keeping them laughing about the funny experiences I had in prison.[5]

Stanley reports that he acquires "respectable" feelings about himself as a result of the powerful effect of Shaw's person. These "respectable" feelings were no doubt sustained by Shaw's consistent contact and expression of interest in Stanley's well-being. In the sequel, Stanley repeatedly expresses gratitude for Shaw's loyalty, concern, and availability. Burgess recognized the essential role of the personal relationship when he noted, "The decisive influence in this time of indecision [first year of treatment] was undeniably the continued contact with Mr. Shaw. . . ."[6] Even though Stanley did not succeed at work or school, he was able to prepare his autobiography and stay out of legal difficulties for an entire year—an accomplishment compared with preceding years. As a result of Shaw's intercession, Stanley seems to become better able to care for himself emotionally and physically and begin to develop as an individual.

The necessity of personal contact was recognized by Shaw in its inclusion in the treatment plan but considered an adjunct to helping Stanley adjust to his new social circumstances (foster-home placement, new neighborhood, and employment). The relationship itself was not seen as a central part of the rehabilitation program:

> During the first two years of the period of treatment, we had personal contact with Stanley at least once a week. Through these contacts it was possible to give him insight into his mental processes, and to assist him in solving many problems which necessarily arose during the course of his adjustment to the new cultural world in which he was placed.[7]

Shaw seemed to know intuitively to include personal contact in his plan but did not recognize this aspect of treatment as an essential one in changing Stanley's behavior. Shaw expertly matched environment to personality but tended to overlook the crucial effect of the *experimentor,* or researcher, on the results. In not recognizing himself as a principle agent in Stanley's development, Shaw practices what Burgess calls a case of *transplantation,* a plan that emphasizes changing social circumstances in the process of rehabilitation. As Shaw stated: "[I]t was decided to place Stanley in an entirely new social situation, and to initiate a plan of treatment adapted, as far as possible, to his particular attitudes and personality."[8]

The importance of the personal link between Shaw and Stanley may be illustrated by the fact that Stanley's most serious adult offense, the attempted hold-up of 1930, coincides with the publication of the autobiography and, therefore, with the termination of the formal treatment relationship and with the conclusion of the project. In the sequel Stanley describes his general state of mind at the time of the incident in terms that coincide with the prevailing economic depression. Losses, in a personal relationship and social status, both possibly contributed to a resurgence of feelings of inferiority in Stanley. He apparently felt helpless and hopeless because he had been fired from a job selling radios door to door, had his furniture repossessed, and was evicted. His wife found work, which was a financial relief but also served to reinforce his feelings of inferiority.

It was in this general frame of mind that he committed the attempted robbery. In the incident itself, deserted by his partner, Stanley seemed to lack the nerve and strength to sustain his actions. After failing to convince the proprietor of his determination by shooting up the place, as a form of intimidation, Stanley surrendered his loaded weapon to the man to await the police. The scene is described as taking place conspicuously in a store with large, glass-front windows on a busy street in the middle of the day. The unintended outcome perhaps suggests that an appeal to Shaw for more formal personal help may have been a hidden motive for the crime. The act had the function of reuniting the two men in that Shaw became reinvolved in the case by arranging bail and working to reduce the charges.

Through three illustrations: earliest recollection, delinquencies, and relationship with Shaw, I have tried to outline a pattern in Stanley's behavior; that is in order to avoid feelings of inferiority he repeatedly reacts by attempting to impress his superiority on others. Although this pattern emerges as a major theme, it is not the only dynamic nor the whole of Stanley's personality. Burgess's identification of "the early rise and persistence of a sense of injustice,"[9] as a "key" personality trait, is related to this theme in that it is this "sense of injustice" that threatens Stanley's feelings of superiority, or respectability, and to which he reacts to avoid feelings of the opposite kind.

This basic pattern appears to be maintained regardless of the social environment in which Stanley is placed. For example, on three occasions in the first book he was informally adopted by affluent and reputable families. In each case, he was unable to manage the feelings of inferiority stirred up in him by the new surroundings. His ability to grasp these opportunities seems to have been precluded by his feelings of personal inadequacy. These same kinds of feelings were rekindled in the foster-home placement arranged by Shaw and expressed when Stanley says he feels like a "pig" in the "parlor" (see chapter 4).

The pattern emerges throughout the sequel and is easier to trace because Stanley, as an older adult, has insight into this pattern in his character. For example, in chapter 4 he reflects on the first treatment year: "My apparent adjustment, however, still revealed a glaring inability on my part regarding relationships with others, especially those with whom I worked. I was often unduly sensitive, carrying a chip on my shoulder, particularly if I fancied myself being imposed upon. I reacted aggresively at critical times which resulted in dismissal."

In chapter 10 he states that the pattern is an enduring part of his character: "Now herein lies the crux of my character regarding others and their impact on my life. When the behavior of others affects me personally I have a rigid code of my own—I simply do not allow anyone to take advantage of me, and there is no compromise. My attitude is such that any violation of my welfare in any way is resisted at the slightest provocation."

Most of the interviews in part III contain illustrations of Stanley's tendency to react aggressively to humiliating experiences and indicate that

the basic pattern persists in adult life. As an example, one of the most
serious incidents is described in chapter 20. Here Stanley became incensed
and violent over the quality of service rendered by a female bartender. He
was treating himself to the best whisky to deal with his feelings concerning
recent occupational and marital failures. Stanley became antagonized when
the woman did not comply with his expectation to be treated as special. He
verbally attacked the bartender, physically assaulted her male companion,
and successfully eluded the police.

One afternoon, Stanley and I discussed his thoughts about an earlier
version of the previous comments, and we had an opportunity to review his
experience in these particular incidents and in general. His reply is quoted at
length as a conclusion because it allows Stanley to act as the ultimate
authority on the personal meaning of his conduct.

I'm trying today to back away from all contention and I find that it's working. I think that I'm overcoming it, but, I will say this, and this is very interesting as far as I'm concerned, the tendency to react is always there. If
I'm prodded, I go off like a cannon. Then I want to react strongly against
anything I feel is unfair. Now whether that's because I'm a Libra or
whether it's because I was pushed around before I was five-six-seven years
old, I don't know. I'm inclined to think so.

I agree with certain authorities that your personal makeup mentally is
established in the early years. I must have had some awful experiences
before I was conscious of them. I look back at it and say to myself, well, I
must have been a pretty bad kid if I was pushed around that much. But
then on the other hand, I couldn't have been *that* bad to be pushed around
that much. I try to understand it, not only from my standpoint, but from
the other side. But, today I have no worries—I'm completely relaxed—
every mood is free—it's a wonderful thing.

Now if anyone ever had influence over me it was Shaw. Occasionally I'd be
disturbed over some certain thing and he would say, "Just forget about it,
don't let it concern you." What concerned me was so overwhelming that it
overshadowed all else, you see? He incorporated a sense of humor into
situations that I would rear up at. He would laugh at them, you see.
Whereas I would be inclined to say, "Who the hell is this guy, I'd like to
punch him in the nose."

You know, I think about it afterwards, and I say to myself, well why all this
turmoil? I agree that this reaction takes place and I don't think that I will
ever overcome it. There may be more guarding against episodes and alter-
cations verbally, and possibly physically. I do have it in mind, but like I
said a moment ago—the reasoning process won't keep pace with the reaction (chuckles). The question is, how much time do I have? I mean, when it
hits me—how much time do I have? Well, there really isn't any time. It
happens so fast that there's only one way, and that's by having it constantly
in my mind. But (chuckles) everyday living precludes that sort of thing.

I will say this. I've found it very efficacious and gratifying to master my
reactions, and afterwards, I'd say, "What a wonderful thing that is." It's

compensating, so it is an inducement, a great inducement! But, (chuckles) I'll tell you (chuckles) that mechanism is built in.

I know that when you're sitting at the gambling table, there are a lot of people that don't like to lose. There are other people it doesn't bother. There are certain people that just *resent* the winner. I find myself sometimes, somebody beats me, and I say to myself, "That son-of-a-bitch, I'm going to get him." And you know what goes on in my mind after that? "don't feel that way, that's wrong! He's trying to win just like you are, you damn fool! Why lose your head about it?" Now, if I can catch myself in these things, I'll have this thing whipped.

I have a hard time restraining myself when I don't think it's fair, see. Yet at the same time, when I get angry, it's not vocally. It's within me. I don't say—I got more class than that. I can lose. I always felt that if you can't be a good loser, you can't be a winner. So anybody that cries in the game, I have no use for them, and I don't do any crying either. It gets in under my craw because, goddamn it, if they can't lose, get up off the table, and that's what I tell them when they get me mad (laughs). If you can't stand to lose, get the hell out of here, because we're all trying to win, see.

Notes

1. Clifford R. Shaw, *The Jack-Roller: A Delinquent Boy's Own Story,* 2nd ed. (Chicago: University of Chicago Press, 1966), p. 54.

2. Ibid., p. 51.

3. Ibid., p. 86.

4. Ibid., p. 57.

5. Ibid., p. 168.

6. Ibid., p. 195.

7. Ibid., pp. 166-167.

8. Ibid., pp. 165-166.

9. Ibid., p. 191.

Postscript

In October 1981 Stanley was hospitalized with a growth near his left eye that was diagnosed as cancerous and removed surgically. He was at home during Christmas and in apparent good spirits, believing that the treatment possibly had been effective. He and Sonia remarried and Stanley was given the Last Rites in the Catholic Church. When we met, he expressed a concern whether the sketchiness of the last chapters of this book portrayed adequately the maturity he felt he had attained in the latter stages of his life. Knowing that we had a publisher, he provided several pages intended as elaboration that turned out to be quite familiar. His conclusion recapitulated the main theme:

> I am no different than most people in that I value acceptance socially. In ending, I would like to dwell on how fortunate I am to have lived through the early traumatic years and yet to have emerged relatively unscathed. There must be protective angels for a boy such as myself that lacked the usual blessings of a home and family. I shall always remember, however, the humble days of adversity, living in the shadow of the horn of plenty.
>
> The fires of passion have long since burned out and today I follow a routine that allows for rather simple requirements. I cannot overemphasize my earnest appreciation for the host of people that have been kind and helpful to me; most of all, my wife Sonia. True enough, I have known of the harsh and seedy, but I have also been gifted by knowing goodness, and I find the difference to my liking. I enjoy peace of mind in the twilight of my life, and I stand without rancor or hate for whatever has happened to me. I am pleased also if, by this publication, I am helpful to Jon Snodgrass, his associates, and to social science.

Stanley was rehospitalized in January 1982 and remained bedridden for months in excruciating pain. He died on 25 April 1982 at the age of seventy-five. He is buried in San Fernando Mission Cemetery, Granada Hills, California.

About the Contributors

Gilbert Geis is professor, Program in Social Ecology, University of California, Irvine. He received the Ph.D. from the University of Wisconsin in 1953. His primary field of research is white-collar crime, and he has written extensively about a wide variety of criminological and legal issues. He is a former president of the American Society of Criminology, and has held visiting appointments at the Institute of Criminology, Cambridge University; Faculty of Law, Sydney University; Harvard Law School; and the School of Criminal Justice, State University of New York, Albany.

Solomon Kobrin is professor emeritus in the Sociology Department, University of Southern California, and senior research associate in its Social Science Research Institute. He was previously a research sociologist on the staff of the Sociology Department, Illinois Institute for Juvenile Research, Chicago, where he was associated with Clifford Shaw and Henry McKay in studies of the social ecology of juvenile delinquency and in the development of neighborhood-based delinquency-prevention programs. During this period he came to know personally many of the subjects of Shaw's biographies of delinquent boys. His current work includes evaluation research on delinquency-control programs, studies of changes in the distribution of crime in urban areas, and studies of the social and political context of crime-control efforts.

James F. Short, Jr., is professor of sociology and director of the Social Research Center, Washington State University. He is currently associate editor of the *Annual Review of Sociology*, was previously editor of the *American Sociological Review*, and has also served in editorial capacities for several other journals and books. He was elected council-at-large member of the American Sociological Association (1968-1970) and was secretary of that association from 1977-1980. Dr. Short was codirector of research for the National Commission on the Causes and Prevention of Violence (1968-1969). He is the coauthor of *Suicide and Homicide: Some Economic, Sociological and Psychological Aspects of Aggression* and *Group Process and Gang Delinquency*, and author of *Delinquency, Crime, and Society* and *The State of Sociology: Problems and Prospects*. Dr. Short has been a Guggenheim Fellow, a Fellow at the Center of Advanced Study in the Behavior Sciences, a Fellow at the Institute of Criminology at Cambridge University, and has held a number of visiting professorships. He received the M.A. and Ph.D. degrees from the University of Chicago. In 1977 he received the Paul W. Tappan Award of the Western Society of Criminology and, in 1979, the Edwin H. Sutherland Award of the American Society of Criminology.

About the Author

Jon Snodgrass is an associate professor of sociology in the Department of Sociology and Social Work, California State University, Los Angeles. He received the Ph.D. from the University of Pennsylvania in 1972. He is registered in California as a research psychoanalyst in training at the Reiss-Davis Child Study Center in West Los Angeles, where he expects to receive the Ph.D. in child psychoanalytic psychotherapy in 1983. He has published articles on the intellectual history of criminology, the feminist mens' movement, and psychoanalysis and sociology. He is editor of *For Men Against Sexism: A Book of Readings* (1976).